# THE
# REVELATION
## *of* JESUS

VERSE BY VERSE BIBLE
COMMENTARY

# THE
# REVELATION
# *of* JESUS

## C. DAVID WRIGHT

XULON PRESS

Xulon Press
2301 Lucien Way #415
Maitland, FL 32751
407.339.4217
www.xulonpress.com

Unless otherwise indicated, Scripture quotations taken from the King James Version (KJV)–*public domain*.

Paperback ISBN-13: 978-1-6628-2258-2
Ebook ISBN-13: 978-1-6628-2259-9

# DEDICATION

To Sylvia, my loving wife, lifelong companion, and favorite listener of many years of Biblical discussions. Without her patient support, this book could not have been written and published.

# TABLE OF CONTENTS

# INTRODUCTION

W E ARE LIVING IN A CHALLENGING TIME IN
America. In time of change, it is vital for every believer to
study the book of Revelation, for every teacher to teach it, and for
every pastor to preach it. Events occurring today provide believers
with more reason than previous generations to believe that the
events prophesied in this book could begin soon. Today is the day
to vigorously study and "rightly divide" this last book of the Bible
(2 Tim. 3:16).

A study of the book of Revelation will convict believers of the
need for holy living, encourage evangelism and missions, and provide hope for the future like no other book of the Bible. In this
prophesy, Jesus shows us the end of the story and believers are on
the winning side.

The goals of this verse-by-verse commentary include:

- Highlighting the great truths of Revelation

- Explaining each verse in terms that are understandable and
  informative

- Leading readers through each problematic, controversial, or
  symbolic passage and the meaning of each

- Suggesting personal and practical application of life-
  changing truths

## CHAPTER 1

# THE PROMISE OF REVELATION

**Revelation 1:1** The Revelation of Jesus Christ, which God gave unto him, to shew unto his servants things which must shortly come to pass; and he sent and signified it by his angel unto his servant John:

THIS FIRST CHAPTER PROVIDES AN INTRODUC-tion to Revelation by answering seven key questions about this book.

**WHO IS THE AUTHOR?** John begins, "The Revelation of Jesus Christ..." This book is not the revelation of "Saint John." It is far more than a revelation of God's prophetic plan. This book is the revelation, the unveiling, and the manifestation of its author: Jesus Christ. Without this book, our understanding of Jesus and our view of who Jesus is will remain incomplete. We love the baby born in a manger. We love the eye-witness accounts of him walking on water and feeding the multitude. We cherish the savior who died on the cross. The Book of Revelation gives us a clear look at Jesus Christ, who alone can open the seven-sealed book of judgment and who will return as King of kings to establish his kingdom on Earth.

Ironside noted:

> The word rendered *revelation*, and sometimes *apocalypse*, means an unveiling, or manifestation. So, this book is the unveiling of our Lord Jesus Christ; He is its one great theme... It is *the* Revelation – one blessed, continuous manifestation of God's unique Son, the anointed Prophet, Priest, and King.[1]

**WHO WAS THE MESSENGER?** The Lord explained, "which God gave unto him..." God the Father gave the message to Jesus, who sent it "by his angel" (verse 2). This is the only book in the Bible so special that Jesus' angel delivered it!

**WHAT IS THE PURPOSE?** "To show unto his servants things which must shortly come to pass." The book of Revelation is the only New Testament book of prophecy. Akin noted,

> In 404 verses, with 285 Old Testament citations and as many as 550 Old Testament allusions, we discover not a closed book but an open book—one to be read and not rejected."[2]

Many prophecies find their ultimate fulfillment in this great book. These things "must shortly come to pass," indicating that they will happen suddenly and without delay once they begin.

**WHO WAS THE WRITER?** The Lord said, "unto his servant John." John was James' brother. They were the sons of Zebedee (Matt. 4:21), two fishermen who worked with Simon Peter (Lu. 5:10). Jesus called them to be among the twelve apostles (Matt. 10:2). John and his brother also asked to be seated on Jesus' left and right in glory (Mark 10:37). They were privileged to see Jesus appear with Moses and Elijah (Matt. 17:1-3). James and John accompanied Jesus to the Garden of Gethsemane (Mark 14:32-33). John became one of three church leaders (Lu. 9:28), wrote the Gospel of John (John 21:24), and three letters entitled 1st, 2nd, and 3rd John.

Most suggest that he was **the last living apostle** at the time of the writing of this book.

> **Revelation 1:2** Who bare record of the word of God, and of the testimony of Jesus Christ, and of all things that he saw.

John explains his role as the writer of Jesus' Revelation:

- **Recording the *logos*:** Revelation is the inspired, infallible Word of God, given to us by the one who is the living Word (Jo. 1:1).

- **Recording Jesus' testimony:** In this New Testament prophecy, Jesus provides testimonial evidence (Rev. 1:9) of the coming judgment as God's wrath is poured out on this Earth (Rev. 11:18; Rev. 16:1).

- **Recording the visions:** The visions John received were from Jesus (Rev. 9:17).

> **Revelation 1:3** Blessed is he that readeth, and they that hear the words of this prophecy, and keep those things which are written therein: for the time is at hand.

**WHY STUDY THIS BOOK?** This verse provides three reasons every believer should commit to a dedicated study of every word in all twenty-two chapters:

- **Revelation is a Promise** – "Blessed is he that readeth..." No other book in the Bible promises a blessing for all who read it, hear it, and keep or observe it.

- **Revelation is a Prophecy** – "and they that hear the words of this prophecy..." This book contains divine predictions regarding the church, the nation of Israel, and many other nations. It also contains prophecies regarding the devil, his evil army, and most importantly, regarding Jesus Christ. The prophetic material about Jesus instructs us about his role in these prophecies, his victory over Satan, and his final judgment of all mankind. These are the most important prophecies in God's Word for the end times!

- **Revelation is Pertinent** – "for the time is at hand." This book gives us hope beyond our current troubles in this world and for the coming tribulations at the end of time. Revelation gives us a bright glimpse of an eternal future with Jesus in a new Heaven and Earth!

## THE POWER OF REVELATION

> **Revelation 1:4** John to the seven churches which are in Asia: Grace be unto you, and peace, from him which is, and which was, and which is to come; and from the seven Spirits which are before his throne;

**WHO RECEIVED THE MESSAGE?** Revelation is addressed "to the seven churches which are in Asia..." A circular trade route began at the Roman province closest to John's island prison, in an area we call Turkey today. Sending this profound book to these first-century churches provided an opportunity for broad circulation and ensured that believers today might read it.

Since this book's intended recipients were Christians in local churches, there is no question regarding the applicability to all believers today.

**WHAT AUTHORITY STANDS BEHIND THE MESSAGE?**

**GOD THE FATHER**
"From him which is, and which was, and which is to come..." When Moses asked what name to give the Israelites, God told him, "I AM THAT I AM..." (Exod. 3:14). The name for God found here in verse four has the same meaning as the "I AM" in Moses' day: "him

which is" (Present), "and which was" (Past), "and which is to come" (Future). Look for this important title again in verse 8.

## GOD THE HOLY SPIRIT

The greeting from the "seven Spirits which are before his throne" is not intended to correct pneumatology (doctrine of the Holy Spirit). There is only one Holy Spirit. Ephesians 4 clearly states, "There is one body, and one Spirit..." (Eph. 4:4). Chapters 4 and 5 mentions "The seven Spirits" again and provide some clarification (Rev. 4:5, 5:6).

> **Revelation 1:5** And from Jesus Christ, who is the faithful witness, and the first begotten of the dead, and the prince of the kings of the earth. Unto him that loved us, and washed us from our sins in his own blood,

**GOD, THE SON** "And from Jesus Christ..."
This book is the Revelation of Jesus Christ. Chapter 1 uses several descriptive names for Jesus that are used throughout the book:

---

### TITLES FOR JESUS IN REVELATION

- Faithful Witness 1:5; 3:14
- First Begotten of the Dead 1:5 (Col. 1:18)
- Prince of the Kings of Earth 1:5
- Lord of Lords and King of Kings 1:5; 17:14; 19:16
- Alpha and Omega, the First and Last 1:8; 1:11; 21:6; 22:13
- Son of Man 1:13; 14:14
- He that Liveth and was Dead Rev. 1:18; 2:8
- Son of God 2:18
- The Amen 3:14
- The Lion of the Tribe of Judah 5:5
- The Root of David 5:5
- The Lamb 5:8, 12, 13; 6:1, 16; 7:9, 10, 14, 17; 12:11; 13:8; 14:1, 10: 15:3; 17:14; 19:7, 9; 21:9, 14, 22, 23, 27; 22:1, 3
- The Word of God 19:13
- The Bright and Morning Star 22:16

---

**Revelation 1:6** And hath made us kings and priests unto God and his Father; to him be glory and dominion for ever and ever. Amen.

The redeemed have a bright future serving the Lord as "kings and priests unto God..." Chapters 5 and 20 emphasize the same phrase, "they shall be priests of God and of Christ, and shall reign with him a thousand years" (Rev. 20:6).

**Revelation 1:7** Behold, he cometh with clouds; and every eye shall see him, and they also which pierced him: and all kindreds of the earth shall wail because of him. Even so, Amen.

One of the main themes of Revelation is found in this verse, "Behold, he cometh..." Although "every eye shall see him" at his second coming, not all welcome Jesus' return. Many will "wail because of him," and some will flee crying "hide us from the face of him that sitteth on the throne, and from the wrath of the Lamb:" (Rev. 6:16).

**Revelation 1:8** I am Alpha and Omega, the beginning and the ending, saith the Lord, which is, and which was, and which is to come, the Almighty.

McGee commented:

From an alphabet you make words, and Jesus is called the 'Word of God' – the full revelation and intelligent communications of God. Jesus is the only alphabet you can use to reach God, my friend. The only language God speaks and understands is the language where Jesus is the Alpha and the Omega and all the letters in between.[3]

These statements in verses 4 and 8 are both about God the Father. Look for similar statements in verse 11 but with a significant twist.

Having concluded his opening greetings, John proceeds to the incredible details of what he saw.

## THE PERSON OF REVELATION

> **Revelation 1:9** I John, who also am your brother, and companion in tribulation, and in the kingdom and patience of Jesus Christ, was in the isle that is called Patmos, for the word of God, and for the testimony of Jesus Christ.

Lea and Black provide us some background, "John stated that he wrote from the island of Patmos, a rugged, rocky island located in the Aegean Sea, forty miles southwest of Ephesus. Roman authorities used the island as a place of exile for offenders and criminals."[4]

Emperor Titus Flavius Domitianus (or Domitian) exiled John to this island around AD 95 to silence John's preaching of the Gospel. According to tradition, John was allowed to return to Ephesus after Emperor Domitian died.

> **Revelation 1:10** I was in the Spirit on the Lord's day, and heard behind me a great voice, as of a trumpet,

The first reference to Sunday as "the Lord's day" is found in this verse.

> **Revelation 1:11** Saying, I am Alpha and Omega, the first and the last: and, What thou seest, write in a book, and send it unto the seven churches which are in Asia; unto Ephesus, and unto Smyrna, and unto Pergamos, and unto Thyatira, and unto Sardis, and unto Philadelphia, and unto Laodicea.

THE REVELATION OF JESUS

The person speaking to John identifies himself with the same title used in verse 8, "I am Alpha and Omega..." However, in the coming verses, John clearly describes the speaker as Jesus, confirming this in verse 18 when he says, "I am he that liveth and was dead." Jesus and the Father are one.

Jesus asked John to send this book to seven churches in Asia. On a clear day, from a high point on Patmos, John could see Asia Minor's shores where the seven churches were located.

The order of these cities listed in this verse begins with Ephesus, the city closest to John's prison. It then follows in a circular clockwise pattern northeastward through the Roman province of Asia Minor, ending with Laodicea. We will learn more about each church as we study the letters Jesus sent to each.

> **Revelation 1:12** And I turned to see the voice that spake with me. And being turned, I saw seven golden candlesticks;

The description of the candlesticks is similar to the golden lamp-stand in the Old Testament. In verse 20, Jesus explains what the seven candles symbolize: "the seven candlesticks which thou sawest are the seven churches."

> **Revelation 1:13** And in the midst of the seven candlesticks one like unto the Son of man, clothed with a garment down to the foot, and girt about the paps with a golden girdle.

In this vision, Jesus appeared, "in the midst of the seven candlesticks..." Jesus has always been among believers, as he promised: "where two or three are gathered together..." (Matt. 18:20). His presence is both an encouragement, and at times when we fail, it is also a sobering truth.

John describes the appearance of Jesus, "one like unto the Son of Man..." Akin notes, "The title goes back to Daniel 7:13-14. This is Jesus' favorite self-designation. It occurs 81 times in the Gospels. It identifies Him as the heavenly Messiah who is also human and who will receive an eternal kingdom."[5]

The description of the resurrected Jesus in the following verses should bring to mind previous post-resurrection appearances of Jesus:

- He appeared to **Stephen** just before he died (Acts 7:56).

- He appeared to **Saul** on the road to Damascus (Acts 9:5).

> **Revelation 1:14** His head and his hairs were white like wool, as white as snow; and his eyes were as a flame of fire;

The image in this verse is parallel to Daniel 7, "the Ancient of days did sit, whose garment was white as snow, and the hair of his head like the pure wool: his throne was like the fiery flame..." (Dan. 7:9). Daniel 7 is a vision of God the Father. Since the original description in the Old Testament vision and this New Testament vision both appear to describe the same person, this again supports the doctrine of the Trinity: **Jesus and the Father are one**.

> **Revelation 1:15** And his feet like unto fine brass, as if they burned in a furnace; and his voice as the sound of many waters.

John compared the sound of Jesus' voice to the mighty roaring of rushing water, "and his voice as the sound of many waters." Ezekiel used the phrase twice to describe Jehovah's voice when he spoke (Ezek. 1:24; 43:2).

> **Revelation 1:16** And he had in his right hand seven stars: and out of his mouth went a sharp

twoedged sword: and his countenance was as the
sun shineth in his strength.

In verse 20, Jesus clarifies the meaning of the seven stars: "The seven stars are the angels of the seven churches." God's Word indicates an angel is assigned to Israel (Dan. 12:1) and that believers have guardian angels (Matt. 18:10). It would be reasonable to conclude that God has appointed an angel over each of his local churches. Walvoord also notes, "Since the word *angel* means 'messenger, one who is sent,' it is best to understand these angels not as divine beings, but as the leaders in these churches who are responsible for their spiritual welfare."[6] With either view, these messengers are in Christ's right hand or under his authority and protection.

The "sharp twoedged sword" will be mentioned again at the second coming of Jesus Christ. "And out of his mouth goeth a sharp sword, that with it he should smite the nations" (Rev. 19:15). Hebrews 4 confirms that the sword pictures the Word of God, "For the word of God is quick, and powerful, and sharper than any twoedged sword" (Heb. 4:12).

John described Jesus' glory, "his countenance was as the sun that shineth." In Revelation chapters 21-22, we read of the brilliance of the glory of Christ in the city that will come down from Heaven. "And the city had no need of the sun, neither of the moon, to shine in it: for the glory of God did lighten it, and the Lamb is the light thereof" (Rev. 21:23).

> **Revelation 1:17** And when I saw him, I fell at his feet as dead. And he laid his right hand upon me, saying unto me, Fear not; I am the first and the last:

Jesus' statement, "I am the first and the last" will be repeated in the letters to the churches (Rev. 2:7), and in the final chapter, "I am Alpha and Omega, the beginning and the end, the first and the last" (Rev. 22:13). Jesus encouraged John with a reminder of his eternal existence. He is first as our Creator when "all things were made by him..." (John 1:3). He will be last when he returns and ultimately "make all things new" (Rev. 21:5).

> **Revelation 1:18** I am he that liveth, and was dead; and, behold, I am alive for evermore, Amen; and have the keys of hell and of death.

There can be no question that the claim, "I am he that liveth, and was dead," could only be made by one person in the history of the world. Jesus Christ alone lived, died, and now lives again eternally.

Holding "the keys of hell and of death" indicate Jesus' authority over the two most feared things by man. Through his resurrection, Jesus took the keys or power over death from Satan. Hebrews explains, "that through death he might destroy him that had the power of death, that is the devil" (Heb. 2:14). Philosophers, scientists, and religious leaders of all ages have sought the keys to life and death. Revelation reveals that Christ alone holds those keys!

## THE PURPOSE OF REVELATION

> **Revelation 1:19** Write the things which thou hast seen, and the things which are, and the things which shall be hereafter;

In this instruction to John, Jesus gives a simple outline for the entire book of Revelation:

- The Past: "Write the things which thou hast seen" – the initial vision of Jesus that John received on Patmos (Chapter 1).

- The Present: "The things which are" – current and prophetic events regarding the churches (Chapters 2-3).

- The Future: "The things which shall be hereafter" – the prophecies of tribulation, Jesus' second coming, and the New Heaven and Earth (Chapters 4-22).

**Revelation 1:20** The mystery of the seven stars which thou sawest in my right hand, and the seven golden candlesticks. The seven stars are the angels of the seven churches: and the seven candlesticks which thou sawest are the seven churches.

Jesus explains "the mystery" regarding several symbols shown to John in this vision. Osborne explained, "It refers to hidden secrets kept from the people of the past but now disclosed by God."[7] What a privilege and blessing to study a book that unveils the most essential mysteries of the ages to come!

As the first verse of this book began, this is "the Revelation of Jesus!" The 22 chapters of Revelation provide **a progressive unveiling of Jesus Christ**:

- **The Son of God** – Jesus rules in Heaven over the church (chapters 1-3).

- **The resurrected Lamb of God** – Only Jesus is worthy to execute judgment on a fallen world under the Antichrist's rule (chapters 4-18).

- **The returning king of kings** – Christ is coming to conquer and establish his reign on Earth (chapters 19-20).

- **The light of the new Heaven and Earth** – The Lord will dwell with his children for eternity (chapters 21-22).

Baxter organized Revelation into three movements about Christ:

In the first movement, covering the first five chapters, the goal is the enthronement of Christ *in heaven*. In the central movement, covering chapters vi.-xx., the goal is the enthronement of Christ *on earth*. In the final movement the lovely climax is the enthronement of Christ *in the new creation.*[8]

McGee also noted that Revelation is a book about Jesus.

> Again let me call your attention to the fact that the Book
> of Revelation is Christocentric, that is, Christ-centered.
> Don't let the four horsemen carry you away, or don't be
> distracted by the blowing of the trumpets or by the seven
> performers. And don't let your interest center on these
> bowls of wrath. Let's keep our eyes centered on Christ.
> He is in charge; He is the Lord. In this book we have the
> unveiling of Jesus Christ in His holiness, in His power,
> and in His glory.[9]

## Lessons from Chapter 1:

- **The Book of Revelation promises a blessing to all who will read it.**

- **The Book of Revelation is a progressive unveiling of Jesus Christ.**

## CHAPTER 1 OUTLINE

I. THE PROMISE OF REVELATION 1-3

   A.  Who is the Author?

   B.  Who is the Messenger? 1

   C.  What is the Purpose? 1

   D.  Who is the Writer? 2

   E.  What Should be Done about the Message? 3

   F.  Why Study It? 3

## II. THE POWER OF REVELATION 4-8

   A.  Who Received the Message? 4

   B.  What Authority Stands Behind the Message? 4-8

## III. THE PERSON OF REVELATION 9-18

   A.  Jesus' Humanity 13

   B.  Jesus' Divinity 14

   C.  Jesus' Authority 15-18

## IV. THE PURPOSE OF REVELATION 19-20

   A.  It is a Record 19

   B.  It is a Revelation 20

# THE SEVEN LETTERS TO THE CHURCHES – PART 1

CHAPTER 2 PROVIDES FOUR OF THE SEVEN letters to the churches in Asia. Each letter includes similar contents:

- Important teachings about Jesus
- First-century conditions believers faced
- Words of praise or areas of need for the church
- A concluding life lesson to remember

The titles this author chose for each church represent what type of churches Jesus wrote to, as well as typical churches existing today.

## THE LOVELESS CHURCH

> **Revelation 2:1** Unto the angel of the church of Ephesus write; These things saith he that holdeth the seven stars in his right hand, who walketh in the midst of the seven golden candlesticks;

Ephesus was a city of 225,000 with two main attractions: a busy seaport and the Temple of Diana (or Artemis), one of the Seven Wonders of the World. The wealth and worldliness of the city made spiritual life quite challenging for first-century believers.

Paul spent three years in Ephesus and built a strong church (cf. Acts 19:11). He wrote a letter to the church from prison in Rome (the book of Ephesians). Thirty years later, the next generation of Christians in the church received this letter by John's hand from Jesus Christ himself.

At the beginning of each of these seven letters, Jesus identifies himself by one of his descriptions from the chapter 1. In this first letter, he chose, "he that holdeth the seven stars..."

> **Revelation 2:2** I know thy works, and thy labour, and thy patience, and how thou canst not bear them which are evil: and thou hast tried them which say they are apostles, and are not, and hast found them liars:

The first chapter pictured Jesus walking amid the churches (Rev. 1:13). He begins each of the seven letters with a reminder: "I know thy works..."

The church of Ephesus was **a defensive church**, keeping "them which are evil" from getting a foothold in their fellowship.

They were also **a discerning church**, testing those who claimed "they are apostles" and exposing deceivers.

> **Revelation 2:3** And hast borne, and hast patience, and for my name's sake hast laboured, and hast not fainted.

The church of Ephesus was a **dedicated church**, having suffered for the name of Christ, been faithful, and had "not fainted."

Following several commendations, Jesus' letter continued with an area of need followed by a warning.

> **Revelation 2:4** Nevertheless I have somewhat against thee, because thou hast left thy first love.

John wrote these letters around AD 95. Thirty years prior, Paul wrote to the church commending them for their love. "After I heard of your faith in the Lord Jesus, and **love unto all the saints**, [16] Cease not to give thanks for you, making mention of you in my prayers" (Eph. 1:15-16). Three decades later, Jesus stated they, "**left thy first love.**" These believers did not lose their love but made a poor choice and left it.

The second generation of believers in Ephesus was zealous, orthodox, and dedicated to the cause of Christ. Yet, they chose to abandon the love they once demonstrated.

Paul taught that without love, the church's service and ministry are of no value (1 Cor. 13:1-3). Walvoord points out:

> Thus it has ever been in the history of the church: first a cooling of spiritual love, then the love of God replaced by a love for the things of the world, with resulting compromise and spiritual corruption. This is followed by departure from the faith and loss of effective spiritual testimony.[10]

> > **Revelation 2:5** Remember therefore from whence thou art fallen, and repent, and do the first works; or else I will come unto thee quickly, and will remove thy candlestick out of his place, except thou repent.

Jesus directed this church to **three steps of restoration**, which are still applicable to believers today:

- **Remember** – The church must remember the previous love and service that pleased the Lord.

- **Repent:** Believers must change the thoughts behind their actions, agreeing with God about their failure and sin. McGee explained the need for repentance:

  Believe me, Christians need to repent. We need to break the shell of self-sufficiency, the crust of conceit, the shield of sophistication, the veneer of vanity, get rid of the false face of 'piosity,' and stop this business of everlastingly polishing our halos as if we were some great saint. Repent! Repentance means to turn back to Him, and it is the message for believers.[11]

- **Return** – God's people must return to doing what pleased the Lord in the beginning.

Jesus is the "head over all things to the church" (Eph. 1:22). He called these believers to repentance and warned, he "will remove thy candlestick." There is some evidence that the church of Ephesus survived at least into the second century. One may conclude that they chose to return to their first love, although it may not have lasted long.

Jesus continued his letter with one additional commendation.

> **Revelation 2:6** But this thou hast, that thou hatest the deeds of the Nicolaitans, which I also hate.

Twice in this chapter, Jesus wrote that he "hated the deeds" and teaching of this group. These beliefs were spread by a sect connected to "Nicolaus a proselyte of Antioch" (Acts 6:5). The Nicolaitans tempted believers to participate in the idolatry and the immoral aspects of its worship. Many are convinced that it is wrong for a Christian to hate; yet twice here in Jesus' letter to this church he said, "which I also hate."

Some believers today choose to avoid taking a stand against evil to prevent accusations of being hateful or judgmental. This first letter from Jesus to one of the early churches records Jesus' commendation for their hatred of this false sect. Verse 15 provides additional comments on "the deeds of the Nicolaitans."

> **Revelation 2:7** He that hath an ear, let him hear what the Spirit saith unto the churches; To him that overcometh will I give to eat of the tree of life, which is in the midst of the paradise of God.

Jesus concludes each of his letters with a call, "He that hath an ear, let him hear..." Osborne comments, "There is also a strong emphasis on the responsibility of God's people to open their ears, and it could be translated, 'Let the one who is willing to hear, listen.'"[12]

At the end of each of the seven letters, Jesus gave a promise to "him that overcometh." In this first letter, Jesus promised that overcomers will "eat of the tree of life." The first book in the Bible explains that the tree of life was originally in the Garden of Eden (Gen. 2:9). Since the fall of man and Adam's expulsion from the garden (Gen. 3:24), the tree of life disappeared. In Revelation's final chapter John describes eternity and said he saw the tree of life "in the midst of the paradise of God" (Rev. 22:2).

Lesson from the Loveless Church:

- **Without love, the service, separation, and sound doctrine all mean nothing.**

## THE LONGSUFFERING CHURCH

> **Revelation 2:8** And unto the angel of the church in Smyrna write; These things saith the first and the last, which was dead, and is alive;

Smyrna was about 35 miles north of Ephesus, a distance considered about one day's journey. It was the second most wealthy city in Asia, located on a natural seaport. Today, it is one of Turkey's largest cities, named Izmir, with a population of 500,000.

At the time of the writing of this letter, worship of Caesar was the central focus of the city. Every street led from the harbor to an ornate Roman temple dedicated to Caesar!

Paul began this church during the three years he spent in Ephesus (cf Acts 19:10).

> **Revelation 2:9** I know thy works, and tribulation, and poverty, (but thou art rich) and I know the blasphemy of them which say they are Jews, and are not, but are the synagogue of Satan.

The church of Smyrna was under "tribulation" for their faith in Jesus Christ. By the time John wrote this letter, the Temple in Jerusalem had been a burnt ruin for over 25 years.

Using the same tactic Jewish religious leaders used against Paul, in Smyrna they stirred up the Roman officials against the Christians until the Romans imprisoned the believers. Once imprisoned, the government confiscated their possessions, leaving them in "poverty." Jesus used a poignant description of their Jewish persecutors: he knew "the blasphemy of them" as a "synagogue of Satan."

> **Revelation 2:10** Fear none of those things which thou shalt suffer: behold, the devil shall cast some of you into prison, that ye may be tried; and ye shall have tribulation ten days: be thou faithful unto death, and I will give thee a crown of life.

The devil has always delighted to use organized religion to fight God's purpose and plans. Smyrna was a complex city for Christians to live out their faith. As the headquarters of the Imperial Cult, at least once a year, everyone was required to come and worship Caesar at the temple in Smyrna or face dire consequences.

Jesus said they would "have tribulation ten days," a common figure of speech indicating a short or limited time. He admonished them, "Be thou faithful unto death..."

Polycarp was one of the early church leaders in Smyrna. He would have been among believers who initially received this letter. Around AD 155, the Romans arrested Polycarp for his faith in Christ. When asked by the Roman proconsul to recant his faith in Christ, he replied, "Eighty and six years have I served him, and he never once wronged me; how then shall I blaspheme my King, Who hath saved me?"[13] Tradition indicates he was burned at the stake in the arena.

Jesus promised, "I will give thee a crown of life." John's brother James, one of the leaders of the first church in Jerusalem, used the same term: "Blessed is the man that endureth temptation: for when he is tried, he shall receive the crown of life..." (James 1:12). Paul wrote about a crown awaiting him, "Henceforth there is laid up for me a crown of righteousness, which the Lord, the righteous judge, shall give me at that day: and not to me only, but unto all them also that love his appearing" (2 Tim. 4:8).

> **Revelation 2:11** He that hath an ear, let him hear what the Spirit saith unto the churches; He that overcometh shall not be hurt of the second death.

To the overcomers in this second letter, Jesus promised they "shall not be hurt of the second death." Revelation 20 explains the meaning of second death: The first death is common to all, a physical death. The second death results from final judgment, ending in an eternal death (Rev. 20:13-14).

The church of Smyrna is one of two churches that received no criticism in their letter from Jesus.

Lessons from the Longsuffering church:

- **Persecution is not unusual for those in God's will.**

- **The Lord expects us to hold fast to the faith, even unto death.**

## THE LEAVENED CHURCH

> **Revelation 2:12** And to the angel of the church in Pergamos write; These things saith he which hath the sharp sword with two edges;

Pergamos was 40 miles north of Smyrna near the Aegean Sea. It was another very wealthy and influential city:

- Pergamos was considered a center of education. A library of 200,000 volumes was sent from Pergamos to Egypt as a gift from Anthony to Cleopatra.

- It was also the center of medicine. There was a temple dedicated to Asclepius, the serpent god of medicine to the Greeks and Romans.

- It was a center of pagan worship. Temples built for to many of the most important Roman gods surrounded the highest hills of this city.

If Ephesus was considered the great political center of Asia Minor, and Smyrna the great commercial center, then Pergamos was the great **religious center**.

> **Revelation 2:13** I know thy works, and where thou dwellest, even where Satan's seat is: and thou holdest fast my name, and hast not denied my faith, even in those days wherein Antipas was my faithful martyr, who was slain among you, where Satan dwelleth.

According to Jesus' message to this church, he called Pergamos the center of "Satan's seat." At the time John sent this letter, there were temples in Pergamos to Apollos (god of the Sun), Dionysus (god of the harvest), and Athena (goddess of wisdom). Pergamos was home to the temples of Aphrodite (goddess of love and beauty), Asclepius (god of medicine), and one of the Seven Wonders of the World: the great altar of Zeus (god of thunder). It should not be a surprise that Jesus chose to refer to this place as **Satan's headquarters**.

Jesus began his letter by commending them, "thou holdest fast my name, and hast not denied my faith..." Jesus mentioned one believer from this church named Antipas, "my faithful martyr." Some historians indicate that Antipas was the leader of the church of Pergamos. He became one of the first martyrs under Roman persecution in Asia.

> **Revelation 2:14** But I have a few things against thee, because thou hast there them that hold the doctrine of Balaam, who taught Balac to cast a stumblingblock before the children of Israel, to eat things sacrificed unto idols, and to commit fornication.

The background to "the doctrine of Balaam" is explained in Numbers 22-31. A Moabite King named Balak hired the prophet Balaam to pronounce a curse on the armies of Israel (Num. 22:6). God turned the curse into a blessing (Num. 23:11). Balaam counseled Balak to have the Moabite women seduce and intermarry with the Israelites. Balaam suggested tempting the Jews to turn to the gods of the Moabites, resulting in God's judgment (Num. 31:15-16).

Jesus opposed those in the church of Pergamos who "hold the doctrine of Balaam." Some in the church were suggesting that they could participate in the local paganism. Recently saved believers were tempted, coming from that pagan system at one of the city's famous temples.

> **Revelation 2:15** So hast thou also them that hold the doctrine of the Nicolaitans, which thing I hate.

In chapter 2, Jesus condemned "the **deeds** of the Nicolaitans" (Rev. 2:6). Here, Jesus rejects the source of their deeds, "the **doctrine** of the Nicolaitans, which thing I hate." Like Balaam, these heretics tempted their fellow believers to participate in immorality, a common part of pagan temple festivals.

The church in Pergamos was a leavened church. It allowed a mixture of true and false teaching and of godly and ungodly practices. Paul warned, "a little leaven leaveneth the whole lump" (1 Cor. 6:6).

> **Revelation 2:16** Repent; or else I will come unto thee quickly, and will fight against them with the sword of my mouth.

As God sent an angel with a sword to stop Balaam (Num. 22:31), so the Lord warned that if the church failed to repent, he will come with a sword "and will fight against them."

> **Revelation 2:17** He that hath an ear, let him hear what the Spirit saith unto the churches; To him that overcometh will I give to eat of the hidden manna, and will give him a white stone, and in the stone a new name written, which no man knoweth saving he that receiveth it.

Jesus promised overcomers will, "eat of the hidden Manna." During the Exodus, manna was a sweet wilderness bread provided from Heaven (Exod. 16:15). Since he referred to this manna as "hidden," he is referring to spiritual sustenance (Matt. 4:4).

Jesus also promised he "will give him a white stone, and in the stone a new name..." First-century jurors used white stones in a court of law. They would drop a black stone into the urn for a vote of guilty, or white stone for a vote of not guilty.

The white stone of the overcomers will have a "new name written." There are two in the New Testament who received new names from Jesus. Jesus renamed Simon after he began following Jesus. His new name was Peter (Jo. 1:40-42). Saul became Paul after he began his first missionary journey (Acts 13:9). The new names were both given to these men at a time of new beginnings. In the next chapter, Jesus will also promise, "I will write upon him my new name" (Rev. 3:12).

The Lord blesses those who are tempted but resist and overcome.

Lessons from the Leavened church:

- **We can't win the world to Jesus by becoming like the world.**

- **A lack of separation in the church will lead to sin in the church.**

- **Satan primarily fights against the church from within the church.**

## THE LIBERAL CHURCH

> **Revelation 2:18** And unto the angel of the church in Thyatira write; These things saith the Son of God, who hath his eyes like unto a flame of fire, and his feet are like fine brass;

Thyatira was a city about 40 miles southeast of Pergamos. Today it is called Akhisar and is located in western Turkey. In John's day, it was a wealthy commercial city known for its red dyes and many trade guilds:

- the potter's guild

- tanner's guild

- weaver's guild

- robe maker's guild

- dyer's guild

To make a living, a tradesman had to join a guild (similar to trade unions). The problem for Christians in Thyatira was that these guilds were known for their pagan social festivals, celebrated with drunkenness and immorality. Members of most guilds were required to participate.

Jesus introduced himself in this verse as "the Son of God," the only time this important term is used in Revelation. Mark this, since **some cults falsely claim that Jesus never claimed He was the Son of God.**

> **Revelation 2:19** I know thy works, and charity, and service, and faith, and thy patience, and thy works; and the last to be more than the first.

The liberal church works, loves, and patiently serves. The liberal church is outwardly impressive, attractive, and appealing. But the fiery eyes of the Lord look beyond the outward appearances and see the inward truth.

> **Revelation 2:20** Notwithstanding I have a few things against thee, because thou sufferest that woman Jezebel, which calleth herself a prophetess, to teach and to seduce my servants to commit fornication, and to eat things sacrificed unto idols.

Note three things the Lord had against this church:

**They were a tolerant church.** There was a woman in the church named Jezebel who "calleth herself a prophetess." Jesus said the church "**sufferest** that woman." They were loving and patient, but the Lord was displeased with their tolerance of this false teacher.

In the Old Testament, Jezebel was a queen in Israel who promoted the worship of Baal led by hundreds of false prophets (See 1 Ki. 18). Here, we find her first-century namesake in this church, and they tolerated her promotion of idolatry.

The tolerance of the liberal church usually requires truth to be sacrificed. Phillips noted the tolerance of our culture:

> We are living in a most tolerant age. Everyone must be allowed to do his own thing. This is the age of relativism in morals and syncretism in religion. There are no absolutes. The spirit of the age has crept into the church. The denouncing of a belief as heresy is to be branded as intolerant. The strongest language in the Bible is reserved for those who depart from revealed truth.[14]

**They were a tempted church.** Jesus stood against this church for allowing the false prophetess, "to teach and to seduce my servants to commit fornication..."

The church in Thyatira was a tolerant church where peace was more valuable than purity. Today, the liberal church accuses other believers of being judgmental, narrow-minded, and unenlightened. Jesus' warning reminds the church to hold the line on truth and purity and stop Jezebel's in the church from misleading God's people.

> **Revelation 2:21** And I gave her space to repent of her fornication; and she repented not.

We often wonder why God does not strike down wickedness the moment it begins. Peter gave a helpful principle that explains the Lord's delay. He explained that the Lord's longsuffering allows people "space to repent" and avoid judgment (2 Pet. 3:9).

> **Revelation 2:22** Behold, I will cast her into a bed, and them that commit adultery with her into great tribulation, except they repent of their deeds.

After her lack of repentance, Jesus will "cast her into a bed," indicating suffering or sickness. He warns that others in the church must also repent to avoid "great tribulation."

> **Revelation 2:23** And I will kill her children with death; and all the churches shall know that I am he which searcheth the reins and hearts: and I will give unto every one of you according to your works.

Jesus reminded that he "searcheth the reins and the hearts." Osborne explained that the readers in John day understood the reins as, "the core of emotions and feelings." He concluded, "Nothing can be hidden from the inquiry of the Lord. Therefore, 'all churches' had better examine their own house, lest the same judgment befall them, for they will not get away with their sins."[15]

> **Revelation 2:24** But unto you I say, and unto the rest in Thyatira, as many as have not this doctrine, and which have not known the depths of Satan, as they speak; I will put upon you none other burden.

**They were also a troubled church.** Jesus describes Jezebel's teachings as the, "depths of Satan." The liberal church is troubled, outwardly walking in spiritual light, but inwardly troubled and tolerating deep spiritual darkness.

> **Revelation 2:25** But that which ye have already hold fast till I come.

Jesus encouraged those in the church who had rejected the false prophetess to "hold fast till I come."

> **Revelation 2:26-27** And he that overcometh, and keepeth my works unto the end, to him will I give power over the nations: [27] And he shall rule them with a rod of iron; as the vessels of a potter shall they be broken to shivers: even as I received of my Father.

Psalm 2 is the basis for this prophecy regarding Jesus' rule over his earthly kingdom: "Thou shalt break them with a rod of iron; thou shalt dash them in pieces like a potter's vessel" (Ps. 2:9) The fulfillment of this prophecy is found in Revelation 19, "And out of his mouth goeth a sharp sword, that with it he should smite the nations: and he shall rule them with a rod of iron..." (Rev. 19:5).

> **Revelation 2:28-29** And I will give him the morning star. [29] He that hath an ear, let him hear what the Spirit saith unto the churches.

The promised gift of "the morning star" will come up again in the final chapter of Revelation, "I Jesus have sent mine angel to testify unto you these things in the churches. I am the root and the offspring of David, and the bright and morning star" (Rev. 22:16).

Lessons from the Liberal church:

- **We can't sacrifice truth for tolerance or purity for peace.**

- **When God withholds judgment, his desire is to allow time for repentance.**

# CHAPTER 2 OUTLINE

## I. THE LOVELESS CHURCH 1-7

## II. THE LONGSUFFERING CHURCH 8-11

## III. THE LEAVENED CHURCH 12-17

    A. The Leavened Church is Impure. 12-14

    B. The Leavened Church is Immoral. 15-17

## IV. THE LIBERAL CHURCH 18-29

    A. The Liberal Church is Tolerant 18-20 a

    B. The Liberal Church is Tempted 20 b-23

    C. The Liberal Church is Troubled 24-29

# THE SEVEN LETTERS TO THE CHURCHES — PART 2

THE THIRD CHAPTER PROVIDES THE LAST three letters from Jesus to the seven churches in Asia Minor.

**THE LIFELESS CHURCH**

> **Revelation 3:1** And unto the angel of the church in Sardis write; These things saith he that hath the seven Spirits of God, and the seven stars; I know thy works, that thou hast a name that thou livest, and art dead.

Sardis was a city about 30 miles southeast of Thyatira and was the former capital of Lydia. A commercial trade route ran through this city which was known for its affluence. The temple of Artemis (goddess of the hunt), a temple to Caesar, and a temple for Cybele worship (mother goddess) were all located in Sardis. Cybele worshippers were known for immoral festivals and for mutilating their bodies in the worship of their pagan goddess.

Evidence shows that this church continued until the fourteenth century. Today, a small town called Sart is located on the original site of this city.

Jesus does not begin this letter with any commendation. Jesus wrote, "thou hast a name," indicating that the church had a reputation in the area. However, Jesus said this church was "dead." The church held meetings and worshipped but had lost its spiritual life, power, and vitality. Stedman nicknamed them "the 'First Zombie Church of Sardis.'"[16]

**The Lifeless church is working.** There may be functions, meetings, services, clubs, outings, and fellowships at the lifeless church. However, routine replaces the leading of the Spirit. In the lifeless church traditions receive preference over needed change, and their focus looks back on the church's glory in the past. The lifeless church convinces itself it is still alive while denying that something within has died.

> **Revelation 3:2** Be watchful, and strengthen the things which remain, that are ready to die: for I have not found thy works perfect before God.

**The lifeless church is weak.** Jesus gave **two solutions** to save the lifeless church. First, they needed to "be watchful." Ladd explained the relevance to this church's location:

> This admonition was particularly relevant in Sardis, for in the city was an impregnable acropolis which had never been seized by frontal attack; twice, however, in the history of the city, the acropolis had been taken by stealth because of lack of vigilance on the part of its defenders.[17]

Jesus also urged the church to "strengthen the things which remain." Everything in the church was not dead yet. The lifeless church focused on the **status quo**. They celebrate the laurels of their past, while the spiritual cancer was killing the little that remained. Their only hope was to reject the status quo, re-focus, and strengthen the few spiritual things still alive in their ministry.

> **Revelation 3:3** Remember therefore how thou hast received and heard, and hold fast, and repent. If therefore thou shalt not watch, I will come on thee as a thief, and thou shalt not know what hour I will come upon thee.

Jesus warned, "I will come on thee as a thief...," a phrase used to describe a lack of necessary awareness. Both Paul and Peter used this term to describe the coming of the day of the Lord (1 Thess. 5:2, 2 Pet. 3:10). Revelation will be use it again in chapter 16 regarding Jesus' second coming (See Rev. 16:15).

> **Revelation 3:4** Thou hast a few names even in Sardis which have not defiled their garments; and they shall walk with me in white: for they are worthy.

Jesus offered them a mixed commendation. He found "a few names even in Sardis," which were undefiled. Jesus explained that the faithful few would walk with him "in white: for they are worthy." Since there were only a few undefiled, most believers in this church were compromised. The destruction of the lifeless church was not caused by persecution from without, but defilement from within.

> **Revelation 3:5-6** He that overcometh, the same shall be clothed in white raiment; and I will not blot out his name out of the book of life, but I will confess his name before my Father, and before his angels. ⁶He that hath an ear, let him hear what the Spirit saith unto the churches.

Jesus describes the overcomers, "clothed in white raiment." Revelation describes several dressed in white indicating purity:

- The twenty-four elders around God's throne are "clothed in white" (Rev. 4:4).

- Those martyred during the tribulation wear white robes (Rev. 6:11, Rev. 7:14).

- The armies from Heaven follow Jesus to the last battle clothed in white (Rev. 19:14).

Jesus gave a second promise to these overcomers, "I **will not blot out his name** out of the **book of life**." Some misuse this verse to teach against eternal security. They argue that if a name in the book of life could be removed there is no security of salvation. Consider some scriptural background to help rightly interpret Jesus' promise.

## CAN WE BE BLOTTED OUT OF THE BOOK OF LIFE?

There are two types of "books of life" in the Bible:

- The book of the living (Psa. 69:28). This was a register of living citizens. After death, the registrar blotted their names from the book. This book has nothing to do with eternal life.

- The Lamb's Book of Life (Rev. 13:8; Rev. 21:27). This is a register of the names of believers destined for eternal life with Jesus Christ.

In verse 5, Jesus did not say he **will** blot out the names of some who were not overcomers. In context, Jesus provided overcomers a word of encouragement. He stated it in the negative for emphasis: "I will **not** blot out his name." This sort of statement does not require that the opposite must be true. It is an example of a *litotes*. Merriam Webster defines this type of descriptive: an "understatement in which an affirmative is expressed by the negative of the contrary."

Chapter 17 states that names of believers have been in the book of life since "the foundation of the world" (Rev. 17:8). At the final judgment, "whosoever was not found written in the book of life was cast into the lake of fire" (Rev. 20:15). See chapter 13 for a special study regarding the Book of Life.

Revelation 3:5 does not suggest that a believer can have their name blotted out of the Book of Life and lose their salvation. Jesus' positive promise does just the opposite: it encourages struggling believers, like those in Smyrna, to look forward to an eternity in robes of white with their names written forever in the "Book of Life."

Lessons from the Lifeless church:

- **We cannot dwell on the success of the past while ignoring the problems of the present.**

- **Persecution from without may test a church, but defilement from within will destroy it.**

## THE LOVED CHURCH

> **Revelation 3:7** And to the angel of the church in Philadelphia write; These things saith he that is holy, he that is true, he that hath the key of David, he that openeth, and no man shutteth; and shutteth, and no man openeth;

Only in this letter, the Lord uses terms to introduce himself from outside of the descriptions in chapter 1. Jesus identified himself to this church as "he that is holy, he that is true." In chapter 6, the martyrs in Heaven will also call him "holy and true" (Rev. 6:10).

Jesus also identified himself with "the key of David." This reference to King David indicates his fulfillment of a prophecy from the book of Isaiah: "And the key of the house of David will I lay upon his shoulder; so he shall open, and none shall shut; and he shall shut, and none shall open" (Isa. 22:22).

Philadelphia was a city located 28 miles south of Sardis. King Philadelphus founded it and the name meant "brotherly love." It was also on the main Roman trade route, which brought great wealth to the city. It was known for rich grape and wine markets and pagan worship of Dionysus, the god of wine. Today the city is called Alasehir.

> **Revelation 3:8** I know thy works: behold, I have set before thee an open door, and no man can shut it: for thou hast a little strength, and hast kept my word, and hast not denied my name.

**The loved church is powerful.** Although they had "little strength," this church had a decisive influence during their persecution. What the Lord calls his children to do, he enables them to be successful. When the Lord opens a door of opportunity, Jesus promises, "no man can shut it." Through a time of opposition with little strength, Jesus provided them a door of opportunity, and these believers had been faithful to serve the Lord and his word.

> **Revelation 3:9** Behold, I will make them of the synagogue of Satan, which say they are Jews, and are not, but do lie; behold, I will make them to come and worship before thy feet, and to know that I have loved thee.

Satan used the open hostility of the Jewish religious leaders toward Christians to destroy many of the early churches. In the Sermon on the Mount, Jesus promised persecuted believers, "Blessed are ye when men shall revile you, and persecute you..." and continued, "Rejoice, and be exceeding glad: for great is your reward in heaven..." (Matt. 5:11-12).

> **Revelation 3:10** Because thou hast kept the word of my patience, I also will keep thee from the hour of temptation, which shall come upon all the world, to try them that dwell upon the earth.

**The loved church is protected.** Jesus promised he would "keep thee from the hour of temptation." The "hour" is not necessarily a reference to a brief time of trouble, as the "ten days" (Rev. 2:10). Here, Jesus prophesied that this trial "shall come upon **all the world**." He states a broader purpose of this trial will be "to try them that dwell upon the earth."

The description of the trial fits the dark years of tribulation described in Revelation chapters 6-19. Matthew recorded Jesus' warning, "For then shall be great tribulation, such as was not since the beginning of the world to this time, no, nor ever shall be" (Matt. 24:21).

> **Revelation 3:11** Behold, I come quickly: hold that fast which thou hast, that no man take thy crown.

Jesus said, "I come quickly." This was written almost 2,000 years ago, so there may be questions regarding this prophecy's accuracy. However, in the context and timing of the future tribulation period (Rev. 3:10), Jesus' second coming will be within days of the closure of that period, the end of the Antichrist's evil reign.

Jesus admonishes this church to "hold fast." Keeping the faith and holding fast are mentioned four times in these letters:

- Jesus praised the church for holding fast to his name (Rev. 2:13).

- Jesus admonished them to "hold fast" against false teaching (Rev. 2:25).

- Jesus encouraged the undefiled to "hold fast" (Rev. 3:3).

- Jesus edified them to "hold fast" through their trials (Rev. 3:11).

Every child of God should take Jesus' admonition to heart when trials test our faith.

> **Revelation 3:12-13** Him that overcometh will I make a pillar in the temple of my God, and he shall go no more out: and I will write upon him the name of my God, and the name of the city of my God, which is new Jerusalem, which cometh down out of heaven from my God: and I will write upon him my new name. ¹³ He that hath an ear, let him hear what the Spirit saith unto the churches.

Jesus promised, "will I make a pillar in the temple of my God." At the time of writing, the Temple in Jerusalem was in ruins. This reference must be to one of the following temples:

- **A rebuilt temple** in Jerusalem during the tribulation days (Rev. 11:1-2). Paul mentioned this when describing the Antichrist, "so that he as God sitteth in the temple of God, shewing himself that he is God" (2 Thess. 2:4).

- **The heavenly temple** mentioned in Rev. 7, "before the throne of God, and serve him day and night in his temple..." (Rev. 7:15, Rev. 11:19). What a great privilege to enjoy the Lord's eternal presence, "and he that sitteth on the throne shall dwell among them."

Jesus mentions three names representing these overcomers in eternity:

- "The name of my God"

- "The name of the city of my God" (new Jerusalem)

- Jesus' new name (Rev. 19:12)

The final chapter of Revelation describes eternal life in the new Jerusalem and envisions this promise, "they shall see his face; and **his name** shall be in their foreheads" (Rev. 22:4).

Lessons from the Loved church:

- **God opens and closes doors of opportunity in our daily walk.**

- **When God opens a door, no man can close it.**

## THE LUKEWARM CHURCH

> **Revelation 3:14** And unto the angel of the church of the Laodiceans write; These things saith the Amen, the faithful and true witness, the beginning of the creation of God;

Laodicea was a city located about 45 miles southeast of Philadelphia. This brings the seven churches full circle, back just 90 miles due east of where Jesus started at Ephesus. The founder of the city, Antiochus II, named it after his wife. The city was the way-station for Syrian-Palestinian exploits to Rome and was famous for its black wool, eye salve, and banking. Laodicea was a wealthy, self-supporting community of very successful businessmen.

This letter contains no commendation, only reproof. Today, both the city and the church are in ruins. Paul asked that Colossae's letter also be read to this church (see Col. 2:16).

Some twist the meaning of the title Jesus chose, "the beginning of the creation of God." Those against Jesus' deity use this verse to suggest that Jesus was the first creation of God and not the Creator. Yet, John began his Gospel with the truth, "All things were made by Him; and without him was not any thing made that was made" (John 1:3). In Colossians 1, Paul also wrote about Jesus as the Creator, "Who is the image of the invisible God, the firstborn of every creature: [16] For by him were all things created, that are in heaven, and that are in earth, visible and invisible..." (Col. 1:15-16).

> **Revelation 3:15** I know thy works, that thou art neither cold nor hot: I would thou wert cold or hot.

**The lukewarm church is compromised.** This church had one foot in the world and another out of it. This half-hearted approach to Christian living undermined the church's ministry: its worship services, evangelism, missions, music, and the preaching and teaching of God's Word.

> **Revelation 3:16** So then because thou art lukewarm, and neither cold nor hot, I will spue thee out of my mouth.

The term "lukewarm" or tepid only appears here in the New Testament. MacArthur noted Laodicea's fascinating background,

> His metaphorical language is drawn from Laodicea's water supply. Because it traveled several miles through an underground aqueduct before reaching the city, the water arrived foul, dirty, and tepid.[18]

Nausea is the Lord's reaction to those who are spiritually lukewarm.

> **Revelation 3:17** Because thou sayest, I am rich, and increased with goods, and have need of nothing; and knowest not that thou art wretched, and miserable, and poor, and blind, and naked:

**The lukewarm church is comfortable.** The members of this church were not aware they had any spiritual need at all. They had the finest medical care through the famous Asclepios Temple School of Medicine. They were living in a wealthy and prosperous city. They appeared to be one of the most successful churches on the coast of Asia. But health and wealth do not necessarily prove that an individual or a church are spiritually where the Lord desires them to be.

**The lukewarm church is confused.** There is a stark contrast between how the Lord saw the church and how the church saw itself. In their estimation, they were wealthy and successful. But the Lord exposed their **spiritual blindness**, "and knowest not that thou are wretched, and miserable, and poor..."

> **Revelation 3:18** I counsel thee to buy of me gold tried in the fire, that thou mayest be rich; and white raiment, that thou mayest be clothed, and that the shame of thy nakedness do not appear; and anoint thine eyes with eyesalve, that thou mayest see.

The riches and righteousness needed by every believer are not found in this world or earned by our effort. In Christ, the believer finds everything required for this life. Jesus admonished them, "I counsel thee to buy of **me**..." Jesus alone is the source of true spiritual riches and righteousness.

This lukewarm church needed "eyesalve, that thou mayest see." Ironically, in the first-century Laodicea was world-famous for their eye-powder called Phrygian powder.

> **Revelation 3:19** As many as I love, I rebuke and chasten: be zealous therefore, and repent.

The church took this letter from Jesus to heart and zealously repented. This church thrived, and in AD 361, a council of the early church fathers held a historic meeting in Laodicea to canonize the Scripture (decide which books to accept into the New Testament). This church is also mentioned in historical records as late as the fourteenth century!

> **Revelation 3:20** Behold, I stand at the door, and knock: if any man hear my voice, and open the door, I will come in to him, and will sup with him, and he with me.

Jesus reminded the lukewarm church, "I stand at the door and knock." What a blessing to these backslidden, nauseating, and compromised Christians. Jesus still knocks on the door of the lukewarm heart. He waits for that renewed invitation for him to enter and restore sweet fellowship. Jesus will never force open that door.

The artist Holman Hunt has a famous painting of Jesus standing at the door and knocking. People said when he painted it, he asked friends to come by and critique it. One friend told him he left out something significant, the door handle. Holman replied, "This door is a picture of the human heart, and the handle is on the inside."[19]

**Revelation 3:21** To him that overcometh will I grant to sit with me in my throne, even as I also overcame, and am set down with my Father in his throne. [22] He that hath an ear, let him hear what the Spirit saith unto the churches.

Lessons from the Lukewarm church:

- **He who stands for nothing will fall for anything and everything.**

- **Being lukewarm about spiritual things is nauseating to the Lord.**

- **Jesus waits at the door of our hearts for us to repent and renew fellowship.**

## CHAPTER 3 OUTLINE

V. THE LIFELESS CHURCH

A. The Lifeless church is Working 1

B. The Lifeless church is Weak 2-6

## VI. THE LOVED CHURCH

A.  The Loved Church is Powerful 8-9

B.  The Loved Church is Protected 10-13

## VII. THE LUKEWARM CHURCH

A.  The Lukewarm Church is Compromised 14-16

B.  The Lukewarm Church is Comfortable 17

C.  The Lukewarm Church is Confused (deceived) 17-22

## CHAPTER 4

# A HEAVENLY INVITATION

**Revelation 4:1** After this I looked, and, behold, a door was opened in heaven: and the first voice which I heard was as it were of a trumpet talking with me; which said, Come up hither, and I will shew thee things which must be hereafter.

THROUGHOUT THE BOOK OF REVELATION, the unfolding visions shift between scenes in Heaven and on Earth. In chapter 4, John saw "a door opened in heaven," leading to the next part of Jesus' vision which will continue through the end of chapter 5. Notice the pattern of shifting locations throughout this prophetic book:

| SCENE LOCATIONS IN REVELATION | | |
|---|---|---|
| Rev. 4-5 | HEAVEN | |
| Rev. 6:1-8 | | EARTH |
| Rev. 6:9-11 | HEAVEN | |
| Rev. 6:12-17 | | EARTH |
| Rev. 7-8:4 | HEAVEN | |
| Rev. 8:5-11:14 | | EARTH |
| Rev. 11:15-12:3 | HEAVEN | |
| Rev. 12:4-6 | | EARTH |
| Rev. 12:7-12 | HEAVEN | |
| Rev. 12:13-14:20 | | EARTH |
| Rev. 15 | HEAVEN | |
| Rev. 16-18 | | EARTH |
| Rev. 19:1-16 | HEAVEN | |
| Rev. 19:17-20:10 | | EARTH |
| Rev. 20:11-21:9 | HEAVEN / NEW HEAVEN | |
| Rev. 21:10-22:21 | | NEW EARTH |

There should be no question to any believer regarding who controls events on this Earth. As believers study this final book of the Bible, it is vital to recognize the connection between heavenly events around God's throne and the response which follows in this world. Jesus taught us to pray, "Thy kingdom come. Thy will be done in earth, as it is in heaven" (Matt. 6:10). The future will never be under man's control. God's will is accomplished in Heaven, and it will be fulfilled upon the Earth. As we take this truth to heart, it is both sobering and encouraging.

John hears the same "great voice" he heard in chapter 1. He takes God's invitation and finds himself in a heavenly scene.

## A VISION OF GOD'S GLORY

> **Revelation 4:2** And immediately I was in the spirit: and, behold, a throne was set in heaven, and one sat on the throne.

The throne of God is referred to eighteen times in chapters 4-5. LaHaye commented about God's throne,

> The throne of God has been considered the fixed center of the universe, the immovable point of reference. Just as the North Star has been the ancient navigators' positional guide because of its fixed position among the stars, so the throne of God is the place of authority and center of God's rulership for the activities of heaven.[20]

Unbelievers do not like the concept of God seated on a sovereign throne, ruling over the entire universe. Despite Satan's desire to take that seat (Isa. 14:13-14), this truth remains an undeniable fact of both Old and New Testaments.

John attempts to describe the person seated on that throne.

> **Revelation 4:3** And he that sat was to look upon like a jasper and a sardine stone: and there was a rainbow round about the throne, in sight like unto an emerald.

John struggled to find fitting words for God's glorious appearance. He wrote that he "was to look upon like..." and mentions three glistening jewels. The first is "like a jasper," a jeweled substance composing the walls and first foundation of the new Jerusalem (see Rev. 21:18-19). Jasper is a transparent stone that glistens with a variety of vivid colors, probably like our diamond today. He also described God's glory as "a sardine stone," which might compare to our ruby.

John never described the physical person on the throne, but only the brightness of God's glory. There is a scriptural reason for this. John wrote in his Gospel, "No man hath seen God at any time..." (Jo. 1:18). Jesus taught that "God is Spirit..." (Jo. 4:24). God's physical form is seen in Jesus. In Ezekiel chapters 1 and 10, he also only describes God's glory on the throne. The glory of God appears like the glow of diamonds, rubies, and a shining rainbow, "like unto an emerald."

There is an interesting Old Testament parallel to these jewels. Mounted on the breastplate of Israel's high priest were twelve stones representing the twelve tribes of Israel. On that breastplate, jasper represented the tribe of the **first** and eldest son of Jacob, the tribe of Reuben (Ex. 28:20). The ruby-red sardine stone represented the **last** and youngest heir of Jacob, the Tribe of Benjamin (Ex. 28:17).

John saw a glistening rainbow "Round about the throne," indicating it encircled God's throne. When flying up above the clouds during a rain shower, if a plane has the sun shining directly behind it, one can see a complete circular rainbow with the shadow of the aircraft in the very center. It is possible that we only see half of the actual appearance of the rainbow God gave after the flood (Gen. 9:13-14).

## A VISION OF GOD'S CHILDREN

> **Revelation 4:4** And round about the throne were four and twenty seats: and upon the seats I saw four and twenty elders sitting, clothed in white raiment; and they had on their heads crowns of gold.

# WHO ARE THE 24 ELDERS?

There are many interpretations regarding the identity of the crowned elders around God's throne. Some suggest they must be angels or heavenly beings, while others interpret them as the church's representatives.

The most informative description of these crowned elders will be coming in the next chapter (Rev. 5:8-10).

Consider the facts we can gather from chapters 4 and 5 about who the elders must be:

- **They are called *elders*.** As first-century Christians read about elders, they would consider them as religious leaders: an elder leader in a city, in the nation of Israel, among the Jewish priests, or in the church.

- **The "crowns of gold" (Rev. 4:4) indicate these elders were kings or rulers.** Revelation 5 confirms, "And hast made us unto our God kings and priests..." (Rev. 5:10). In the first chapter, John indicated that believers would be "kings and priests unto God and his Father..." (Rev. 1:6). In chapter 20, John describes the earthly reign of Jesus Christ and the fulfillment of this promise, "they shall be priests of God and of Christ and shall reign with him a thousand years" (Rev 20:6).

- **The words of the elders' song.** "And hast redeemed us unto God by thy blood..." (Rev. 5:9). Their song indicates that the elders were **representatives of those redeemed** to God by Jesus' blood. Since they were among the redeemed, they could not be angels as some suggest.

- **These elders came "out of every kindred, and tongue, and people, and nation..."** (Rev. 5:9). Some suggest their number, **twenty-four** must represent the twelve tribes and twelve apostles. Others insist they represent the church. There is insufficient scriptural support to determine who the twenty-four elders may be. The author suggests that the twenty-four crowned elders are glorified believers, representing all of the redeemed before God's throne.

What an amazing truth that God shares the glory of Christ with his children!

## A VISION OF GOD'S POWER

> **Revelation 4:5** And out of the throne proceeded lightnings and thunderings and voices: and there were seven lamps of fire burning before the throne, which are the seven Spirits of God.

The "lightnings and thunderings" are similar to Exodus 20, when God descended on Mount Sinai to give the ten commandments. "And all the people saw the thunderings, and the lightnings, and the noise of the trumpet, and the mountain smoking" (Exod. 20:18). Flashes of lightning and thunderings are recorded three additional times in Revelation (Rev. 8:5, 11:19, and 16:18). Each time they coincide with **God's judgment.**

The "seven Spirits of God" were first mentioned in the Holy Spirit's greeting (Rev. 1:4). Here, the Holy Spirit appears to John before God's throne as "seven lamps of fire." Fire also represented the presence of the Holy Spirit on the Day of Pentecost (Acts 2). Luke described the occasion just before the disciples were all filled with the Holy Spirit, "there appeared unto them cloven tongues like as of fire, and it sat upon each of them" (Acts 2:3). The fire represents the Spirit of God. The number seven does not indicate that there is more than one Holy Spirit but symbolizes the totality, perfection, or completeness of the Spirit.

## A VISION OF GOD'S SERVANTS

> **Revelation 4:6** And before the throne there was a sea of glass like unto crystal: and in the midst of the throne, and round about the throne, were four beasts full of eyes before and behind.

The crystalline "sea of glass" will come up again in chapter 15, "a sea of glass mingled with fire" (Rev. 15:2). The final chapter of Revelation offers several additional details, "And he showed me **a pure river of water of life**, clear as crystal, proceeding out of the throne of God and of the Lamb" (Rev. 22:1). The "pure river of water of life," flows from God's throne and forms the sea of glass.

John continues his description of the "four beasts full of eyes..." These heavenly creatures watchfully serve in God's throne room. The ancient Latin idiom, "having eyes in back of their head" is accurate regarding these heavenly creatures.

> **Revelation 4:7** And the first beast was like a lion, and the second beast like a calf, and the third beast had a face as a man, and the fourth beast was like a flying eagle.

Ezekiel's vision provides background on these beings. He calls them "four living creatures" (Ezek. 1:5). Ezekiel similarly describes their unusual facial features, "As for the likeness of their faces, they four had the face of a man, and the face of a lion, on the right side: and they four had the face of an ox on the left side; they four also had the face of an eagle" (Ezek. 1:10). In chapter ten, Ezekiel received a subsequent vision of God's throne and saw these same four living creatures. In this second vision, he called them *cherubim*: "This is the living creature that I saw under the God of Israel by the river of Chebar; and I knew that they were the cherubims" (Ezek. 10:20).

> **Revelation 4:8** And the four beasts had each of them six wings about him; and they were full of eyes within: and they rest not day and night, saying, Holy, holy, holy, Lord God Almighty, which was, and is, and is to come.

These cherubim praise the holiness of God "day and night."

> **Revelation 4:9** And when those beasts give glory and honour and thanks to him that sat on the throne, who liveth for ever and ever,

There are three references to thanksgiving in Revelation (Rev. 4:9; 7:12, 11:17). All three are praise that occurs in God's throne-room in Heaven. This first one gives thanks to God as our creator.

> **Revelation 4:10** The four and twenty elders fall down before him that sat on the throne, and worship him that liveth for ever and ever, and cast their crowns before the throne, saying,

The elders "cast their crowns before the throne," reminding believers that true worship is humble, seeking only to glorify God.

> **Revelation 4:11** Thou art worthy, O Lord, to receive glory and honour and power: for thou hast created all things, and for thy pleasure they are and were created.

God has "created all things" for his pleasure. Throughout the seven days of creation, Genesis records that "God saw that *it was* good" (Gen. 1:10, 12, 18, 21, 25). God created the mighty cherubim to serve in his throne room for his pleasure (Rev. 4:6). It was for God's pleasure that God created the Earth, the Moon, and the stars and fixed them in space (Gen. 1:16). On the six day, God created man in His image and likeness for his divine pleasure (Gen. 1:26).

Paul wrote that all things were created by God and **for him**. "For by him were all things created, that are in heaven, and that are in earth, visible and invisible, whether they be thrones, or dominions, or principalities, or powers: all things were created by him, and for him" (Col. 1:16).

Lessons from Chapter 4:

- **God plans to share the glory of Christ with his children.**
- **True worship is humble, seeking only to glorify God.**

## CHAPTER 4 OUTLINE

I. A HEAVENLY INVITATION 1

II. A HEAVENLY VISION 2-8

    A.  A Vision of God's Glory 2-3

    B.  A Vision of God's Children 4

    C.  A Vision of God's Power 5

    D.  A Vision of God's Servants 6-8

III. HEAVENLY WORSHIP 9-11

    A.  Heavenly Worship is Thankful 9

    B.  Heavenly Worship is Humble 10

    C.  Heavenly Worship is Honorable 11

# CHAPTER 5

# THE SEVEN-SEALED BOOK

CHAPTER 4 UNVEILED JOHN'S HEAVENLY invitation, the 24 elders, and the powerful cherubim. Chapter 5 continues by introducing the seven-sealed book. The majority of the remaining chapters of Revelation will deal with the contents of this prophetic book (Chap. 6-19).

## THE HEAVENLY DECREE

> **Revelation 5:1** And I saw in the right hand of him that sat on the throne a book written within and on the backside, sealed with seven seals.

In John's day, they did not have flat-bound paper books but wrote on rolls of papyrus or vellum (parchment). This scroll is "written within and on the backside." Scribes normally only wrote on the smooth side. A scroll written on both sides would be very unusual. Ladd explained, "This was not a common practice in the ancient world but was sometimes done; such a book was called an opisthograph."[21]

The scroll was "sealed with seven seals," prohibiting any from reading its contents. There would be a seal on the outside of the entire scroll. When a scribe broke the outer seal, the whole scroll could be read, if there were no other inner seals. This scroll had six additional inner seals preventing that. God's seven-sealed scroll opened to a certain point and stopped at the next inner seal. The wills of Emperor Vespasian and Caesar Augustus also had multiple seals. These rulers also secured their scrolls with seven seals.

There is another sealed-up Old Testament prophecy about the end times. In Daniel 12, the prophet was recording all that God revealed to him. At one point, he was ordered to stop writing. "But thou, O Daniel, shut up the words, and seal the book, even to **the time of the end**: many shall run to and fro, and knowledge shall be increased" (Dan. 12:4). Daniel's prophetic vision was never disclosed but was sealed and kept for "the time of the end..." That phrase suggests that God gave him a prophesy meant for the end times, such as this New Testament prophecy we call the Book of Revelation.

> **Revelation 5:2** And I saw a strong angel proclaiming with a loud voice, Who is worthy to open the book, and to loose the seals thereof?

The mighty angel shouted a question to all in Heaven, "who is worthy?" Notice that he did not cry out, who is powerful? or who is wise? but rather, "who is worthy?"

Revelation demonstrates that this heavenly scroll contains divine decrees of the outpouring of God's wrath on this Earth.

To be worthy to break the seals on this sacred scroll and unleash the long-awaited judgment of God, one must be worthy to judge man and this world. The Gospel of John explained, "For the Father judgeth no man, but hath committed all judgment unto the Son" (Jo. 5:22). God has given the judgment of this world over to only one person.

> **Revelation 5:3-4** And no man in heaven, nor in earth, neither under the earth, was able to open the book, neither to look thereon. ⁴ And I wept

much, because no man was found worthy to open
and to read the book, neither to look thereon.

John recorded that "no man" anywhere was found worthy, and he
wept as he received this news. Akin noted:

> For a brief moment a survey of heaven reveals no one
> possesses the merit to approach God, take the scroll,
> and usher in the eschaton. Not Abraham or Moses. Not
> Joshua or Caleb. Not Elijah or Elisha. Not Jeremiah,
> Ezekiel, or Daniel. Not James, Peter, or Paul. Not an
> angel or even an archangel. A universal search is made.
> No one is worthy.[22]

## THE HEAVENLY REDEEMER

One of the twenty-four elders stepped over to encourage the apostle.

> **Revelation 5:5** And one of the elders saith unto
> me, Weep not: behold, the Lion of the tribe of
> Juda, the Root of David, hath prevailed to open
> the book, and to loose the seven seals thereof.

## THE WONDER OF THE LAMB

Just before his death, Jacob pronounced his final blessings on
Judah: "Judah is **a lion's whelp**: from the prey, my son, thou art
gone up: he stooped down, he couched as a lion, and as an old
lion; who shall rouse him up?" (Gen. 49:9). Jacob prophetically
saw Judah as the Lion among his twelve sons. Jesus fulfilled that
ancient prophesy and became "the Lion of the tribe of Juda."

A prophecy in Isaiah also provides background for the second title,
"And in that day there shall be **a root of Jesse**, which shall stand for
an ensign of the people; to it shall the Gentiles seek: and his rest
shall be glorious" (Isa. 11:10). A root or offspring of King David's

father, Jesse, is Jesus. He will one day bring glorious restoration to Israel.

These two Old Testament titles for Jesus demonstrate:

- Jesus Christ fulfills all the unfulfilled prophecies about the coming Messiah.
- During the days of the tribulation, the second coming, and the millennial kingdom, Israel will again become the center of God's focus.

God keeps all his word and will never break one promise he has made.

> **Revelation 5:6** And I beheld, and, lo, in the midst of the throne and of the four beasts, and in the midst of the elders, stood a Lamb as it had been slain, having seven horns and seven eyes, which are the seven Spirits of God sent forth into all the earth.

John turned to see the Lion of Judah in the center of this heavenly crowd, and he saw Jesus, "a Lamb as it had been slain." The symbol of Jesus as the Lamb of God will appear ten times in 12 of the chapters of Revelation. The Lamb was the first title John the Baptist gave to Jesus. "Behold **the Lamb of God**, which taketh away the sin of the world" (John 1:29).

John gives some unusual details about the vision of the Lamb. He noted that the Lamb appeared "as it had been slain." John could see the scars, the crucifixion marks. Ironside noted:

> When He came forth from the tomb the print of the nails was there. When John saw Him many years after in vision up there in glory, he saw a Lamb that looked as though it had once been offered in sacrifice; and

when we get home to heaven we will never make any mistake in identifying Him."[23]

The vision of the Lamb also had "seven horns and seven eyes." The horn is a common Old Testament symbol of power and rule. The symbol of seven horns on the Lamb represents the **omnipotence of Jesus.** Ephesians 1 declares:

> What *is* the exceeding greatness of his power to us-ward who believe, according to the working of his mighty power, [20] Which he wrought in Christ, when he raised him from the dead, and set *him* at his own right hand in the heavenly *places,* [21] **Far above all principality, and power, and might**, and dominion, and every name that is named, not only in this world, but also in that which is to come: (Eph. 1:19-21).

Verse 6 explains that the seven eyes are "the seven Spirits of God." Chapters 1, 3, and 4, showed that is a representation of the Holy Spirit. Akin notes, "This description is nothing less than a full affirmation of the Lamb's deity, for only God is all-powerful, all knowing, and everywhere present."[24]

> **Revelation 5:7-8** And he came and took the book out of the right hand of him that sat upon the throne. [8] And when he had taken the book, the four beasts and four and twenty elders fell down before the Lamb, having every one of them harps, and golden vials full of odours, which are the prayers of saints.

Jesus alone is worthy to take the seven-sealed book out of God's "right hand." The response of the cherubim and elders is to bow and worship him.

The elders have "golden vials" which contain "the prayers of saints." Chapter 8 reveals the extraordinary plan God has for these collected prayers (Rev. 8:3-4). As a child of God, we should realize our prayer requests may be treasured in golden vials in Heaven.

## THE WORTHINESS OF THE LAMB

> **Revelation 5:9** And they sung a new song, saying, Thou art worthy to take the book, and to open the seals thereof: for thou wast slain, and hast redeemed us to God by thy blood out of every kindred, and tongue, and people, and nation;

Jesus alone is found worthy to open this book of final judgment. Jesus shed his blood on the cross and offered salvation to sinful man. MacArthur comments on the blood of Christ.

> At the cross, the Lord Jesus Christ paid the purchase price (His blood; 1 Pet. 1:18-19) to redeem men from every tribe (descent) and tongue (language) and people (race) and nation (culture) from the slave market of sin (cf. 1 Cor. 6:20; 7:23; Gal. 3:13).[25]

> **Revelation 5:10** And hast made us unto our God kings and priests: and we shall reign on the earth.

Although the elders wore crowns they will not rule over Heaven. They "shall reign on the earth" with Jesus during his millennial kingdom. Chapter 20 provides those details (Rev. 20:4).

## THE WORSHIP OF THE LAMB

> **Revelation 5:11** And I beheld, and I heard the voice of many angels round about the throne and the beasts and the elders: and the number of them was ten thousand times ten thousand, and thousands of thousands;

John heard "the voice of many angels." He may have tried numbering them, but he only provider a broad count, "Ten thousand times ten thousand." According to the math, this represents **100 million**. Then John added for good measure, "and thousands of thousands." This description pictures millions of heavenly angels surrounding God's throne.

> **Revelation 5:12** Saying with a loud voice, Worthy is the Lamb that was slain to receive power, and riches, and wisdom, and strength, and honour, and glory, and blessing.

The countless crowd of angels is joined by the four cherubim and twenty-four elders shouting, "Worthy is the Lamb that was slain..." Imagine the joyous sound of such praise by this heavenly multitude.

> **Revelation 5:13** And every creature which is in heaven, and on the earth, and under the earth, and such as are in the sea, and all that are in them, heard I saying, Blessing, and honour, and glory, and power, be unto him that sitteth upon the throne, and unto the Lamb for ever and ever.

Paul wrote to the church in Philippi, "That at the name of Jesus every knee should bow, of things in heaven, and things in earth, and things under the earth; [11] And that every tongue should confess that Jesus Christ is Lord, to the glory of God the Father" (Phil. 2:10-11). Note that Paul used the same groupings as John: in Heaven, in Earth, and under the Earth.

> **Revelation 5:14** And the four beasts said, Amen. And the four and twenty elders fell down and worshipped him that liveth for ever and ever.

The four cherubim who began chapter 4 with their cries of "Holy, Holy, Holy..." (Rev. 4:8), now close this praise to God and the Lamb with a heavenly "Amen."

This chapter celebrates that Jesus alone will be found worthy. We are surrounded by a self-centered society, believing they deserve everyone's attention. Such narcissism thinks, "it is all about me." According to their worldview, everything revolves around their wealth, power, and prideful attempts at attaining personal glory. This passage exposes a sobering truth: It is **not** all about us; **it is all about Jesus**! He alone will be found worthy.

Lessons from Chapter 5:

- **God keeps his word and will fulfill every promise he has ever made.**

- **The perspective of most is self-centered, "it is all about me." A day is coming when all the world will discover: It is all about Jesus!**

## CHAPTER 5 OUTLINE

IV. A HEAVENLY DECREE 1-4

V. THE HEAVENLY REDEEMER 5-14

    A. The Wonder of the Lamb 5-8

    B. The Worthiness of the Lamb 9-10

    C. The Worship of the Lamb 11-14

# CHAPTER 6

# THE SEVEN SEALS OF JUDGMENT

CHAPTERS 4-5 SERVE AS AN INTRODUCTION to the outpouring of God's wrath during the end-times. Chapter 6 explains six of the seven seals of judgment. When the seventh seal is broken, it will reveal seven additional trumpet judgments.

| STAGES OF JUDGMENT IN REVELATION | | |
|---|---|---|
| SEVEN SEAL JUDGMENTS | | |
| 1st SEAL (Chapter 6) | | |
| 2nd SEAL | | |
| 3RD SEAL | | |
| 4TH SEAL | | |
| 5TH SEAL | | |
| 6TH SEAL | | |
| 7TH SEAL . . . . . . . . . . . . . . . . | SEVEN TRUMPET JUDGMENTS | |
| | 1ST TRUMPET (Chapter 8) | |
| | 2nd TRUMPET | |
| | 3RD TRUMPET | |
| | 4TH TRUMPET | |
| | 5TH TRUMPET | |
| | 6TH TRUMPET . . . . . . . . . . . . | *(Seven Thunders, Ch. 10) |
| | 7TH TRUMPET . . . . . . . . . . . . | SEVEN VIAL JUDGMENTS |
| | | 1st VIAL (Chapter 16) |
| | | 2nd VIAL |
| | | 3RD VIAL |
| | | 4TH VIAL |
| | | 5TH VIAL |
| | | 6TH VIAL |
| | | 7TH VIAL |

The gradual unveiling of these judgments allows the viewer to see farther ahead into the distance, like expanding sections of an ancient telescope. The seven-sealed book, once completely opened, contains a total of twenty-six stages of judgment.

## SEVEN SEALS OF JUDGMENT

### THE SEAL OF DOMINATION

> **Revelation 6:1-2** And I saw when the Lamb opened one of the seals, and I heard, as it were the noise of thunder, one of the four beasts saying, Come and see. ² And I saw, and behold a white horse: and he that sat on him had a bow; and a crown was given unto him: and he went forth conquering, and to conquer.

As Jesus breaks the first seal on the book, **the seven-year tribulation begins**. The first four seals reveal the "four horsemen of the apocalypse." Verse 2 describes a conqueror riding on "a white horse." In the vision, this rider appears to be like Christ, mounted on a white horse with a crown. However, this is all a deception. This rider will be the false Messiah we call the Antichrist. The type of "crown" given to this horseman is that of the **victor**. The crown Jesus will wear at his second coming will be a *diadem* which is that of a **sovereign** or King of kings (Rev. 19:12).

Daniel is the sister-book to Revelation and provides some of the most important Old Testament background. Daniel also prophesied about the coming false Messiah:

> And after threescore and two weeks shall Messiah be cut off, but not for himself: and the people **of the prince that shall come** shall destroy the city and the sanctuary; and the end thereof shall be with a flood,

and unto the end of the war desolations are determined (Dan. 9:26).

The rider John saw had "a bow" but no arrows. The false Messiah will be **given** his worldwide rule after signing a peace treaty or what Daniel refers to as a covenant. "And he shall confirm the covenant with many for one week" (Dan. 9:27). Daniel 11 also explains that the Antichrist will use deceit to establish his initial rule. "And in his estate shall stand up a vile person, to whom they shall not give the honour of the kingdom: but he shall come in peaceably, and obtain the kingdom **by flatteries**" (Dan. 11:21). The first horseman represents **the rise of the Antichrist.**

## THE SEAL OF DESTRUCTION

> **Revelation 6:3-4** And when he had opened the second seal, I heard the second beast say, Come and see. ⁴ And there went out another horse that was red: and power was given to him that sat thereon to take peace from the earth, and that they should kill one another: and there was given unto him a great sword.

The second horsemen will ride a red horse of war with a "great sword," representing the war and bloodshed to come. The deceitful treaties and promises of peace at the beginning of the Antichrist's reign will be disingenuous and short-lived. This second rider's purpose is "to take peace from the earth." Jesus warned about the end times, "And ye shall hear of wars and rumours of wars: see that ye be not troubled: for all these things must come to pass, but the end is not yet" (Matt. 24:6). **The second horseman represents war.**

## THE SEAL OF DEARTH

> **Revelation 6:5** And when he had opened the third seal, I heard the third beast say, Come and

see. And I beheld, and lo a black horse; and he
that sat on him had a pair of balances in his hand.

This third horseman enters the vision on "a black horse." Black is
typically symbolic of famine (see Jer. 4:28, Lam. 4:8-9). The rider
carries "a pair of balances" symbolizing shortages of food which
will cause the famine. In John's day, balances or scales were used
at the agora (an outdoor market) to measure out the grain. Food
shortages will be expected during the early years of the tribulation.
A heavenly voice portrays this truth in the verse 6.

> **Revelation 6:6** And I heard a voice in the midst
> of the four beasts say, A measure of wheat for a
> penny, and three measures of barley for a penny;
> and see thou hurt not the oil and the wine.

Illustrating the impact of food shortages, the voice of the Lord
announces price-gouging on staple food products. Freeman
explained the meaning of a measure. "The *choenix* 'measure,' was an
Attic dry measure and was nearly equivalent to one quart English.
Its measurement was the usual daily allowance for a soldier or
a slave."[26] The penny was equal to an entire day's wage. Imagine
spending one day's pay for just enough bread to feed one person
for a day. We should keep in mind that this is not uncommon today
in many parts of our world.

The Lord commands that the "oil and wine" be protected.
McGee wrote:

> The oil and wine are luxuries that are enjoyed by the
> rich. Oil would correspond to our toiletries, the beauty
> aids and the body conditioners that we use today; that
> is, the luxuries of life. The wine corresponds to the
> liquor that will be in abundance.[27]

The Antichrist will come to power with false promises of peace and
economic prosperity. In a short time, the new reality will become

worldwide war, food shortages, and famine. **This third horseman represents worldwide famine**.

## THE SEAL OF DEATH

> **Revelation 6:7-8** And when he had opened the fourth seal, I heard the voice of the fourth beast say, Come and see. [8] And I looked, and behold a pale horse: and his name that sat on him was Death, and Hell followed with him. And power was given unto them over the fourth part of the earth, to kill with sword, and with hunger, and with death, and with the beasts of the earth.

The fourth horseman rides a "pale" horse. The original Greek word translated "pale" describes the transparency of **a rotting corpse**. The color befits his name, which is "Death." His partner "Hell" will follow him. MacArthur wrote:

> Death on a massive scale is the inevitable consequence of widespread war and famine. In this macabre and terrifying scene, John saw Hades... following with Death. Hades (here representing the grave) becomes, as it were, the grave digger, burying the remains of Death's victims.[28]

John received a staggering prophecy that "the fourth part" of the world's population will die due to war, hunger, sickness, and attacks from wild animals. To understand the number of deaths, consider our current world population. According to the USCB (United States Census Bureau), the world's population (in 2020) was 7.67 Billion. The death of 25% of the population would amount to a staggering **1.91 billion people**, more than the population of China and the US combined! Jesus said this is only "the beginning of sorrows" (Matt. 24:8). **This fourth horseman represents the death of billions**.

## THE SEAL OF DEFENDERS

> **Revelation 6:9** And when he had opened the fifth seal, I saw under the altar the souls of them that were slain for the word of God, and for the testimony which they held:

John turns his attention back to Heaven, where he noticed an unusual gathering. He saw many martyrs who were "slain for the word of God." It will not be easy to reject the Antichrist and choose to become a Christian. Those who refuse to take the mark of the beast (Rev. 13:14) or bow to his statue (Rev. 13:15) will be under a death sentence. These martyrs are slain "for the word of God," and for holding fast to their faith, just like Antipas of Pergamos (Rev. 2:13).

As the church grows ever closer to the beginning of these dark events, we must ask ourselves if we would be willing to stand for our faith, even at the cost of our lives. What an inspiring testimony of faith to find that these tribulation believers will face such a time and still **choose Jesus**!

> **Revelation 6:10** And they cried with a loud voice, saying, How long, O Lord, holy and true, dost thou not judge and avenge our blood on them that dwell on the earth?

Murdered for their unwavering faith, the martyrs ask, "How long, O Lord..." They see God's justice delayed and wonder about the delay. Such questions are common among believers even today. We wonder why evil seems to go unpunished and why righteousness seems unrewarded. We find the answer to the martyrs' question given in verse 11.

> **Revelation 6:11** And white robes were given unto every one of them; and it was said unto them, that they should rest yet for a little season, until

their fellowservants also and their brethren, that
should be killed as they were, should be fulfilled.

The delay in judgment was part of God's plan, allowing time for
the martyrs to be joined by "their fellowservants also and their
brethren." In the second half of the Antichrist's reign, many more
believers are martyred. We will find their deaths described in chapters 11, 12, 14, and 20.

As the second coming of Christ draws closer, believers should
realize that many of our friends, loved ones, and family members
may put off trusting in Jesus. As the Antichrist rises to power, the
eyes of many will finally be opened. Most who believe will soon
die for their faith in Jesus.

After the end of the seven-year tribulation, Jesus returns and his
earthly reign will begin. John describes what God showed him
about the bright future.

> And I saw the souls of them that were beheaded for the
> witness of Jesus, and for the word of God, and which
> had not worshipped the beast, neither his image, nei-
> ther had received his mark upon their foreheads, or in
> their hands; and they lived and reigned with Christ a
> thousand years (Rev. 20:4).

The martyrs will be resurrected to live and reign with Christ. This
promise provides hope that many will need during the severe
testing to come. **The fifth seal is that of martyrs for the faith.**

**THE SEAL OF DISASTER**

> **Revelation 6:12** And I beheld when he had
> opened the sixth seal, and, lo, there was a great
> earthquake; and the sun became black as sack-
> cloth of hair, and the moon became as blood;

The "great earthquake" prophesied here is the first of several quakes in Revelation (see Rev. 11:13; 16:18-19). The largest recorded earthquake occurred on May 22, 1960, in Chile. It was a magnitude 9.5 (Mw) and resulted in the death of almost 2,000 people. Over 2 million Chileans were left homeless, and the aftershocks caused devastation in Hawaii, Japan, the Philippines, and even the west coast of the United States. Imagine the devastation caused by an even greater quake.

Some suggest that "the sun became black," may describe a solar eclipse. However, a solar eclipse would not cause the moon to shine blood red.

Previous scientific record suggests that volcanic eruptions would account for these effects on both the sun and the moon. The Royal Society has a record of the 1883 eruption of Krakatoa in Indonesia. Smoke blotted the sun from view, and the moon rose and fell behind a colored haze. Detonations rattled windows up to 150 miles away, a 150-foot-high tsunami wave destroyed several cities, killing over 36,000 people.[29]

This chapter's supernatural quake will shake the entire Earth, activating volcanoes worldwide, and filling the Earth's atmosphere with lava and ash (see Isa. 13:9-10; 34:2-4; Joel 2:30-31).

> **Revelation 6:13** And the stars of heaven fell unto the earth, even as a fig tree casteth her untimely figs, when she is shaken of a mighty wind.

John described "the stars of heaven" falling, which may refer to meteor showers. MacArthur notes:

> Modern experts believe that the impacts of asteroids, comets, and meteors striking the earth would be devastating and cause unprecedented destruction. There will be so many such bodies hitting the earth that John,

in vivid analogy, likens the scene to a fig tree that casts its unripe figs when shaken by a great wind.[30]

> **Revelation 6:14** And the heaven departed as a scroll when it is rolled together; and every mountain and island were moved out of their places.

John saw the sky "departed as a scroll when it is rolled together." It will seem like God is rending or tearing the heavens (Isa. 64:1).

Unlike typical quakes with a limited area of impact, this earthquake judgment will cause catastrophic worldwide results: "every mountain and island were moved out of their places." This quake will shake mountains from Mount Everest in the Himalayas, Mount McKinley in Alaska, and Mount Kilimanjaro in Africa. It will destroy resort towns and villages, mining, wildlife, and many ancient forests. The supernatural quake will shake Islands from Hawaii, New Guinea, and the Caribbean. Tropical paradises will be devastated with their beautiful vacation areas, valuable shipping, and unique tropical forests.

Joel also prophesied these destructive events, "And I will show wonders in the heavens and in the earth, blood, and fire, and pillars of smoke. [31] The sun shall be turned into darkness, and the moon into blood, before the great and the terrible day of the LORD come" (Joel 2:30-31).

Jesus warned his disciples, "For nation shall rise against nation, and kingdom against kingdom: and there shall be famines, and pestilences, and earthquakes, in divers places" (Matt. 24:7).

> **Revelation 6:15** And the kings of the earth, and the great men, and the rich men, and the chief captains, and the mighty men, and every bondman, and every free man, hid themselves in the dens and in the rocks of the mountains;

From the highest ruling class of society to the lowest and most common, fear will capture the hearts and minds of all those under God's wrath. They will try to hide from God's wrath. However, the words of the Psalmist provide a reminder:

> Whither shall I go from thy spirit? or whither shall I flee from thy presence? [8] If I ascend up into heaven, thou art there: if I make my bed in hell, behold, thou art there. [11] If I say, Surely the darkness shall cover me; even the night shall be light about me. [12] Yea, the darkness hideth not from thee; but the night shineth as the day: the darkness and the light are both alike to thee (Ps. 139:7,8,11,12).

**Revelation 6:16** And said to the mountains and rocks, Fall on us, and hide us from the face of him that sitteth on the throne, and from the wrath of the Lamb:

Most believers hope that those living through such catastrophic events will be convicted of their sin, recognize God's wrath, and humbly repent. However, John shows us that man tends to embrace **fear rather than faith**. Osborne wrote, "All of these will also be united in their fear. Terror is a great equalizer, and all social distinctions drop away in light of the shaking of the heavens and the arrival of the terrible judgment of God."[31]

**Revelation 6:17** For the great day of his wrath is come; and who shall be able to stand?

In their fear, these unbelievers ask a timely question, "Who shall be able to stand?" Chapter 6 only reveals the first six of twenty-six stages of judgment! When God's wrath is finally ended, the only hope left for life on this Earth will be Jesus' second coming.

Verse 17 names this time as "the great day of his wrath." Throughout God's Word, the day of wrath is a Biblical term for the tribulation period, especially the second half which is called the great tribulation (Zeph. 1:14-16; Dan. 9:20-27; Matt. 24:15).

Almost 800 years before Jesus gave John this vision, Isaiah prophesied similar events. He called this time **the day of the Lord**.

> Behold, the day of the LORD cometh, cruel both with wrath and fierce anger, to lay the land desolate: and he shall destroy the sinners thereof out of it. [10] For **the stars** of heaven and the constellations thereof shall not give their light: **the sun** shall be darkened in his going forth, and **the moon** shall not cause her light to shine. [11] And I will punish the world for their evil, and the wicked for their iniquity; and I will cause the arrogancy of the proud to cease, and will lay low the haughtiness of the terrible. [13] Therefore I will **shake the heavens**, and **the earth** shall remove out of her place, in the wrath of the LORD of hosts, and in the day of his fierce anger (Isa. 13:9-11, 13).

Some interpret many of these judgments symbolically, painting a much different picture of man's future. Jesus warned his disciples about the coming of a great tribulation period for Israel. Matthew chapters 24 and 25 are a parallel prophecy to the judgments of Revelation 6. Jesus' description and grammar do not suggest symbolism. Therefore, the author has taken a more literal interpretive approach to these judgments, following the context provided by Jesus. As the chart demonstrates, the details are parallel to those given here in Revelation 6:

| MATTHEW 24 | REVELATION 6 |
|---|---|
| War 6-7 | War 3-4 |
| Famine 7 | Famine 5-6 |
| Death 7-9 | Death 7-8 |
| Martyrdom 9-10 | Martyrdom 9-11 |
| Signs in the Sky 29 | Signs in the Sky 12-14 |
| Time of Divine Judgment 24:32-25:46 | Time of Divine Judgment 15-17 |

Jesus' prophecy describes literal prophetic events. The parallel prophecy found here in Revelation 6 should also be interpreted as **real future events**.

Lessons from Chapter 6:

- **The question is not if there is life after death, but where will that life be spent.**

- **By the end of the judgments, the only hope left for life on this Earth will be Jesus' second coming.**

# CHAPTER 6 OUTLINE

SEVEN SEALS OF JUDGMENT

   I.  THE SEAL OF DOMINATION 1-2

  II.  THE SEAL OF DESTRUCTION 3-4

 III. THE SEAL OF DEARTH 5-6

 IV. THE SEAL OF DEATH 7-8

  V.  THE SEAL OF DEFENDERS 9-11

 VI. THE SEAL OF DISASTER 12-17

# THE SEALING OF THE 144,000

CHAPTER 6 EXPLAINS SIX OF THE SEVEN seals and John described the judgments contained in each:

- The rise of the Antichrist

- War

- Worldwide Famine

- The death of 25% of the World's population

- Martyrs of the early tribulation

- Every island and mountain are moved out of their place by a supernatural earthquake.

Chapter 7 is the first of several interludes in the dramatic action. This provides a parenthetical pause in the progression of the main account.

This chapter also introduces the 144,000. These protected believers are messianic Jews, born again by their faith in Jesus Christ as their Messiah.

> **Revelation 7:1** And after these things I saw four angels standing on the four corners of the earth,

holding the four winds of the earth, that the wind should not blow on the earth, nor on the sea, nor on any tree.

John sees these four angels standing at each point of the compass: north, south, east, and west. They are preventing the "four winds of the earth" from blowing. Verses 2 and 3 explain the reason.

> **Revelation 7:2-3** And I saw another angel ascending from the east, having the seal of the living God: and he cried with a loud voice to the four angels, to whom it was given to hurt the earth and the sea, ³ Saying, Hurt not the earth, neither the sea, nor the trees, till we have sealed the servants of our God in their foreheads.

The angel carrying "the seal of the living God" (Rev. 7:2) has ordered the four angels to hold back the coming judgment, protecting "the servants of our God." God's grace is so amazing! Even amid the final judgments, God stops everything to protect his faithful servants.

Recall other times God halted judgment until one of his servants was safe:

- God warned Noah and his family about the coming judgment on the Earth and waited for 100 years as Noah built the Ark (Gen. 5:23, Gen. 7:6). As the rain began to fall, God sealed Noah and his family inside the Ark (Gen. 7:1,16,23).

- God sent angels to find Lot, and they held back the fiery judgment on Sodom & Gomorrah until he was safe (Gen. 19:15-16).

> **Revelation 7:4** And I heard the number of them which were sealed: and there were sealed an hundred and forty and four thousand of all the tribes of the children of Israel.

The "seal of the living God" has two primary purposes:

## A Seal of Protection

In chapter 9, John warns about demonic locusts flying out of the bottomless pit (Rev. 9:1-3). These demons are commanded not to hurt those who God had protected. "Only those men which have not the seal of God in their foreheads." One purpose of God's seal is to protect the 144,000 from coming judgments, such as the torture and eventual death caused by the demonic locusts.

## A Seal of Possession

In chapter 14, John describes a bright future after the great tribulation. The vision shows the 144,000 standing on Mount Zion with Jesus. They are described "having his Father's name written in their foreheads" (Rev. 14:1). The "seal of the living God" (Rev. 7:2), like the signet ring of many great rulers, contains a name: "**his Father's name**." God will stamp his seal upon his 144,000 faithful servants to protect them, and that seal will bear the name of God, indicating they belong to him. What a contrast with the worshippers of the Antichrist who will also receive a name or number on their forehead (Rev. 13:17).

Several groups misinterpret the meaning of the 144,000. Charles T. Russell was the Watchtower Bible and Tract Society founder, later renamed the Jehovah's Witnesses. Reed explained Russell's teaching about the 144,000, "This gathering of the 144,000 began at Pentecost in the first century and continued through the year 1935—at which time the number was complete and the door was closed."[32] Other groups similarly suggest that the 144,000 will only include those faithful to their organization's beliefs and practices. These groups all blindly disregard the last seven words of verse 4, "of all the tribes of the children of Israel." **All 144,000 will be Jews!**

**Revelation 7:5-8** Of the tribe of Juda were sealed twelve thousand. Of the tribe of Reuben were sealed twelve thousand. Of the tribe of Gad were sealed twelve thousand. ⁶ Of the tribe of Aser were sealed twelve thousand. Of the tribe of Nepthalim were sealed twelve thousand. Of the tribe of Manasses were sealed twelve thousand. ⁷ Of the tribe of Simeon were sealed twelve thousand. Of the tribe of Levi were sealed twelve thousand. Of the tribe of Issachar were sealed twelve thousand. ⁸ Of the tribe of Zabulon were sealed twelve thousand. Of the tribe of Joseph were sealed twelve thousand. Of the tribe of Benjamin were sealed twelve thousand.

This list of the twelve tribes varies from others in the Bible:

- **Judah** leads the list (Rev. 7:5). Reuben normally begins the list of the twelve tribes as Jacob's firstborn son. Revelation is Jesus' prophecy, and he was from of the Tribe of Judah, a descendant of King David (Matt. 1:1, 1:17). Judah heads this list.

- **Levi** (Rev. 7:7) was one of Jacob's twelve sons but there was not a Tribe of Levi. The Levites served as priests and lived in the Promised Land on land donated by each of the other tribes (Josh. 21:3).

- **Joseph** was one of Jacob's sons, but he is usually represented among the twelve tribes by his two sons: Ephraim and Manasseh (Gen. 49). The Tribe of Manasseh appears in this tribulation list (Rev 7:6), but Ephraim is replaced by Joseph.

- The tribe of **Dan** is missing from the list. The scripture does not explain this exception. Some point to the fact that the Tribe of Dan embraced apostasy and idolatry during the Judges Period (Judg. 18).

> **Revelation 7:9-10** After this I beheld, and, lo, a great multitude, which no man could number, of all nations, and kindreds, and people, and tongues, stood before the throne, and before the Lamb, clothed with white robes, and palms in their hands; [10] And cried with a loud voice, saying, Salvation to our God which sitteth upon the throne, and unto the Lamb.

John begins with the transitional phrase, "After this..." At the conclusion of the seven letters, he used this same transition. The scene has changed from the Earth where the 144,000 were sealed, back to Heaven "before the throne." The timing of this scene is after the great tribulation has ended.

The "great multitude, which no man could number" includes believers from "all nations, and kindreds, and people." Christians from every corner of the world will wear the white robes of Christ's righteousness – the robe of the redeemed.

Freeman explains the use of "palms in their hands."

> Conquerors in the Grecian games returned to their homes triumphantly waving palm-branches in their hands. Thus, in the new Jerusalem John sees the triumphant followers of the Messiah with 'palms in their hands.[33]

They will raise the "palms in their hands," symbolizing the Lord's victory. Their celebration is joined by angels, elders, and the four great cherubim.

> **Revelation 7:11-12** And all the angels stood round about the throne, and about the elders and the four beasts, and fell before the throne on their faces, and worshipped God, [12] Saying, Amen: Blessing, and glory, and wisdom, and

thanksgiving, and honour, and power, and might,
be unto our God for ever and ever. Amen.

The seven-fold praise stirs up a heavenly "Amen." Following this praise, one of the twenty-four elders spoke with John about the great multitude's identity.

> **Revelation 7:13-14** And one of the elders answered, saying unto me, What are these which are arrayed in white robes? and whence came they? [14] And I said unto him, Sir, thou knowest. And he said to me, These are they which came out of great tribulation, and have washed their robes, and made them white in the blood of the Lamb.

John wisely responded to the elder's question, "Sir, thou knowest." The elder explained that this multitude "**came out of great tribulation**." This heavenly scene takes place after Jesus' returns and begins his earthly reign. Their robes will be washed white by "the blood of the Lamb," evidence that this multitude of **tribulation believers is from all four corners of the world**.

We should not miss the connection of these born-again martyrs with the 144,000 from the twelve tribes of Israel (Rev. 7:2-8). God powerfully uses these divinely protected Jewish evangelists to lead an innumerable multitude of souls to salvation during the darkest days on Earth!

> **Revelation 7:15** Therefore are they before the throne of God, and serve him day and night in his temple: and he that sitteth on the throne shall dwell among them.

Their service "day and night in his temple" point ahead to Christ's earthly kingdom (Rev. 20:4-6). John later describes eternity in a new Heaven and Earth without any Temple, "And I saw no temple therein: for the Lord God Almighty and the Lamb are the temple of it" (Rev. 21:22). The elder continues explaining the comforting future ahead for these martyrs of the faith.

> **Revelation 7:16-17** They shall hunger no more, neither thirst any more; neither shall the sun light on them, nor any heat. [17] For the Lamb which is in the midst of the throne shall feed them, and shall lead them unto living fountains of waters: and God shall wipe away all tears from their eyes.

These verses prophesy the beginnings of eternity (Rev. 22:1-5). The famine experienced on Earth under the Antichrist's persecution is forgotten as Jesus "shall feed them" (Rev. 22:2). Their thirst under the blistering heat of the final judgments (Rev. 16:9), is remembered no longer, as he leads them to "living fountains of water" (Rev. 22:1).

Joel also prophesied Israel's pivotal role during the tribulation:

> And it shall come to pass afterward, that I will pour out my spirit upon all flesh; and **your sons and your daughters** shall prophesy, your old men shall dream dreams, your young men shall see visions: [29] And also upon the servants and upon the handmaids in those days will I pour out my spirit. [30] And I will show wonders in the heavens and in the earth, blood, and fire, and pillars of smoke. [31] The sun shall be turned into darkness, and the moon into blood, before the great and the terrible day of the LORD come (Joel 2:28-31).

Paul wrote about Israel's salvation:

> For I would not, brethren, that ye should be ignorant of this mystery, lest ye should be wise in your own conceits; that blindness in part is happened to Israel, until the fulness of the Gentiles be come in. [26] And so **all Israel shall be saved**: as it is written, There shall come

out of Sion the Deliverer, and shall turn away ungod-
liness from Jacob: (Rom. 11:25-26).

Paul acknowledged that the mystery of the church occurred due to
the temporary blindness of the Jews. God has never permanently
rejected the Jews nor denied them any future with the Lord. He
prophesied that a day is coming when "the Deliverer" will turn
Israel back to the Lord, and they will be saved.

McGee comments on those who suggest God is through with Israel:

> There is a system of theology abroad today that passes
> as conservative, but it takes the position that God is
> through with the nation Israel, that all of God's cove-
> nants with Israel are negated, that God does not intend
> to make good any of His promises to Israel—yet there
> are literally hundreds of them in the Old Testament.
> This theological system simply spiritualizes these
> promises, and the proponents do so with no scriptural
> grounds whatsoever.[34]

All that God has promised, he will do without exception. God
keeps his word.

**144,000 spirit-filled Messianic Jews** will shake our world. Under
God's seal of protection, they will give a powerful Gospel witness,
leading multitudes from around the tribulation world to saving
faith in Jesus Christ.

Lessons from Chapter 7:

- **The 144,000 will be spirit-filled, divinely protected,
  Messianic Jews.**

- **Divinely protected messianic Jews are powerfully used
  by God to evangelize an innumerable multitude of souls
  during the darkest days on Earth!**

# OUTLINE OF CHAPTER 7

1. PAUSE IN THE STORM 1-2

2. PROTECTION BY SEALING 3-8

   A.  The Seal of Protection

   B.  The Seal of Possession

3. PRAISE FOR SALVATION 9-12

4. PERSECUTED SERVANTS 13-17

   A.  Their past 14

   B.  Their present 15

   C.  Their future 15-17

## CHAPTER 8

# THE SEVEN TRUMPET JUDGMENTS, PART 1

CHAPTER 7 PAUSED THE ACTION UNTIL THE 144,000 servants were protected. Chapter 8 records the breaking of the final seal on the seven-sealed book.

> **Revelation 8:1** And when he had opened the seventh seal, there was silence in heaven about the space of half an hour.

### Seal of Doom

The contents of the final section begin with the seven trumpet judgments.

Someone said *silence is golden*, but this "silence in heaven" will not be an occasion of celebration. Heaven is a busy place and may not have been silent since the beginning of creation (see Rev. 4:8). Like the silence in a court when the foreman of the jury stands to read the verdict, all Heaven stand silently in awe awaiting the announcement of God's final wrath upon our Christ-hating world.

Dr. Ironside wrote, "He will judge according to the holiness of His character and the righteousness of His throne. The seventh seal introduces the final drama of the Great Tribulation."[35]

> **Revelation 8:2** And I saw the seven angels which stood before God; and to them were given seven trumpets.

Gabriel may be one of these seven angels "which stood before God." When he introduced himself to Mary, he said, "I am Gabriel, that stand in the presence of God" (Lu. 1:19). Ephesians 6 indicates there are ranks of demons, including principalities, powers, and rulers of darkness (Eph. 6:12). There are also ranks of heavenly angels. The "seven angels" in this verse may be archangels. If this is correct, another would be the archangel Michael (see Dan. 12:1).

> **Revelation 8:3-4** And another angel came and stood at the altar, having a golden censer; and there was given unto him much incense, that he should offer it with the prayers of all saints upon the golden altar which was before the throne. [4]And the smoke of the incense, which came with the prayers of the saints, ascended up before God out of the angel's hand.

Once a year, on the Day of Atonement, the high priest carried a censer into the holy place. He scooped incense from the golden altar and took it through the veil into the holy of holies.

On "the golden altar" in Heaven, this angel used the censer to offer incense mixed with "the prayers of all saints." The fragrant smoke will fill God's Heavenly Temple. We should never underestimate the value God places on prayer. Spoken from our hearts, interceded by the Spirit, our prayers may one day be part of this prophetic event.

The angel took up the censer again.

> **Revelation 8:5** And the angel took the censer, and filled it with fire of the altar, and cast it into the earth: and there were voices, and thunderings, and lightnings, and an earthquake.

Following the fire cast "into the earth," John heard and saw something ominous: "voices, and thunderings, and lightnings, and an earthquake." The sights and sounds reveal a pattern in these prophecies:

- John described this in the vision of God's heavenly throne (Rev. 4:5), and the sights and sounds came from the area of his throne.

- It will occur again after the seventh trumpet is sounded (Rev. 11:15), and the sounds will come from the Temple of God.

- The last occurrence will be after the seventh vial of wrath is poured out (Rev. 16:18), and again, the sounds will also come from the Temple of God.

Each of these events are connected with the outpouring of God's wrath.

**Trump of Desolation**

> **Revelation 8:6-7** And the seven angels which had the seven trumpets prepared themselves to sound. [7] The first angel sounded, and there followed hail and fire mingled with blood, and they were cast upon the earth: and the third part of trees was burnt up, and all green grass was burnt up.

Osbourne wrote about the use of trumpets in this book. "In Revelation trumpets are used as symbols of eschatological promise (1:10; 4:1) as well as harbingers of judgment (all the other trumpet blasts occur in connection to the seven judgements here)."[36]

Some do not interpret these plagues as literal events. However, similar judgments during the Exodus indicate a symbolic approach is **not** required. The plagues in Moses' day gives us a reliable model for interpretation. A plague of "hail and fire" was recorded falling upon Egypt:

> And the hail smote throughout all the land of Egypt all that was in the field, both man and beast; and the hail smote every herb of the field, and brake **every tree** of the field. 26 Only in the land of Goshen, where the children of Israel were, was there no hail (Exod. 9:25-26).

The destruction of one-third of the trees and "all green grass" will devastate housing construction, and cause soil erosion. The fire, smoke, and loss of trees will also degrade air quality.

**Trump of Defilement**

> **Revelation 8:8-9** And the second angel sounded, and as it were a great mountain burning with fire was cast into the sea: and the third part of the sea became blood; 9 And the third part of the creatures which were in the sea, and had life, died; and the third part of the ships were destroyed.

John was shown a "great mountain burning with fire," which fits the description of a giant meteor falling through Earth's atmosphere. Several scientists have warned of such a possibility and the devastating aftermath.

John indicates this meteor will fall into the seas, turning the water into "blood." During the Exodus, the Nile River also turned to blood:

> And Moses and Aaron did so, as the LORD commanded; and he lifted up the rod, and smote the waters that were in the river, in the sight of Pharaoh, and in the sight of his servants; and **all the waters that were in**

**the river were turned to blood.** ²¹ And the fish that was in the river died; and the river stank, and the Egyptians could not drink of the water of the river; and there was blood throughout all the land of Egypt (Exod. 7:20-21).

The record in Exodus indicates we should not interpret symbolically, but as a real event.

Pollution of one-third of the seas will result in ecological disaster on an immense scale. It will impact the fishing industry, naval vessels and their cargo, and the import and export of goods worldwide. As of 2019, there were 53,000 merchant ships and another 3,000 naval ships. The loss of one-third of the vessels today would indicate over 16,000 ships, the crews and cargo all lost.

**Trump of Draught**

> **Revelation 8:10-11** And the third angel sounded, and there fell a great star from heaven, burning as it were a lamp, and it fell upon the third part of the rivers, and upon the fountains of waters; ¹¹ And the name of the star is called Wormwood: and the third part of the waters became wormwood; and many men died of the waters, because they were made bitter.

John saw "a great star from heaven" which could be another meteor or a comet, falling through the atmosphere "burning as it were a lamp."

The comet is named "Wormwood," a common herb in the Middle East and one of the bitterest herbs known to man. The painful poisoning of freshwater will result in the deaths of "many men."

Scientists have considered the impact of a comet on Earth. M.I.T. astronomers have determined the atmospheric consequences of a comet impact. The extreme shock as it enters the atmosphere causes a breakdown of oxygen and nitrogen molecules, causing a chemical reaction producing acid rain. A large comet would cause global dispersal of acid rain, weathering the soil, washing insoluble elements into the water, rivers, and lakes. This would be very toxic to plants and animals (See a report by Trevor Palmer entitled, *Perilous Planet Earth*).

John indicates that this judgment will be on "the rivers, and upon the fountains of waters." The loss of one-third of the world's freshwater would cause many deaths, loss of livestock, destruction of many animals, and the failure of crops.

**Trump of Darkness**

> **Revelation 8:12** And the fourth angel sounded, and the third part of the sun was smitten, and the third part of the moon, and the third part of the stars; so as the third part of them was darkened, and the day shone not for a third part of it, and the night likewise.

During the exodus, a plague of darkness was also experienced. The Egyptians endured three days of darkness, and Moses recorded the darkness as very real, "even darkness which may be felt" (see Exod. 10:21-22).

The judgment on "the third part of the sun" will cause temperatures to plummet, resulting in global cooling, crop failures, and famine. In areas without power, the loss of reflective light for a third of the night will leave parts of the world in total darkness.

> **Revelation 8:13** And I beheld, and heard an angel flying through the midst of heaven, saying with a loud voice, Woe, woe, woe, to the inhabiters of the earth by reason of the other voices of the trumpet of the three angels, which are yet to sound!

The three woes each anticipate the devastating impact of the next three trumpet judgments. They also draw attention to the fact that the visions are moving past the midpoint of the tribulation period, into the beginning of the great tribulation.

Lessons from Chapter 8:

- **Someone said silence is golden, but the silence in Heaven in Revelation 8:1 ominously leads to the final devastating judgments of the day of the Lord.**

- **The plagues in Egypt recorded in Exodus were not figurative, and the trumpet judgments are similar. These judgments should be considered real events.**

## CHAPTER 8 OUTLINE

VI. Seal of Doom 1-5

    A.  Trump of Desolation 6

    B.  Trump of Defilement 7-9

    C.  Trump of Draught 10-11

    D.  Trump of Darkness 12-13

# CHAPTER 9

# THE SEVEN TRUMPET JUDGMENTS, PART 2

CHAPTER 9 PROVIDES A GLIMPSE INTO THE unseen spiritual battle in our world. Elisha prayed and asked the Lord to show his servant the angels surrounding their enemies (2 Ki. 6:17). John records a future when usually unseen demonic forces will openly unleash the judgment of God.

**Trump of Demons**

> **Revelation 9:1** And the fifth angel sounded, and I saw a star fall from heaven unto the earth: and to him was given the key of the bottomless pit.

John saw a "star fall from heaven." Most stars are much larger than the Earth or our Sun, so we do not expect a literal star to fall. John also used a personal pronoun for this star "to **him**," indicating that this star is not a meteor but is an intelligent being.

The star will come from Heaven with "the key of the bottomless pit." Chapter 20 records the second visit of this guardian angel: "And I saw an angel come down from heaven, having the key of the bottomless pit..." (Rev. 20:1).

The original word translated "bottomless pit" is *ab'ysos,* from which we get our word "abyss." This pit is mentioned three times here, as well as in three additional chapters to come:

- The Beast (Antichrist) will come from this pit (Rev. 11:7, 17:8).

- Satan will be bound in this pit for a thousand years (Rev. 20:1, 20:3).

> **Revelation 9:2** And he opened the bottomless pit; and there arose a smoke out of the pit, as the smoke of a great furnace; and the sun and the air were darkened by reason of the smoke of the pit.

When the guardian opened the abyss, John saw "smoke out of the pit" darken the sun and the air. Some demons are loose on the Earth, while God keeps others locked away. Peter also wrote about fallen angels waiting in chains of darkness. "For if God spared not the angels that sinned, but cast them down to hell, and delivered them into chains of darkness, to be reserved unto judgment" (2 Pet. 2:4).

Combs wrote about the spiritual unseen world around us:

> Notice there is an interplay between the coexistent and contemporaneous spiritual realm, where Satan and his angels function, as well as God's angels, and the material realm, which we humans see. There is a visible world and an invisible world side by side in God's universe, another dimension undetected by scientific investigations, but nevertheless real, present and inescapable. In this book the interplay between the two realms is most evident.[37]

Like other prophecies in God's Word, the Lord occasionally pulls back the veil on the spiritual world, allowing readers a glimpse into the unseen to help understand what God sees.

> **Revelation 9:3** And there came out of the smoke locusts upon the earth: and unto them was given power, as the scorpions of the earth have power.

The parallel with the ten plagues in Egypt continues in this fifth judgment with "locusts upon the earth" (Ex. 10:12-15). However, these are demonic locusts with "power" in their tail like a scorpion.

> **Revelation 9:4** And it was commanded them that they should not hurt the grass of the earth, neither any green thing, neither any tree; but only those men which have not the seal of God in their foreheads.

These demons are restricted from hurting "the grass of the earth" or any trees. They are also forbidden from harming any of the 144,000. They are sent only to torment those "which have not the seal of God in their forehead." Chapter seven explained that the 144,000 from the twelve tribes are sealed by God (Rev. 7:3-8), under his protection.

> **Revelation 9:5** And to them it was given that they should not kill them, but that they should be tormented five months: and their torment was as the torment of a scorpion, when he striketh a man.

The sting of these demonic creatures will cause torturous pain, "that they should be tormented five months." The next verse describes their response to five months of demonic attack.

> **Revelation 9:6** And in those days shall men seek death, and shall not find it; and shall desire to die, and death shall flee from them.

Those stung by these locust-scorpions "seek death," but are unable to end their pain and suffering. During Jesus' ministry, he also dealt with several under demonic attack who had suicidal tendencies. The father of the demon-possessed child explained to Jesus that his son often tried to kill himself. "And ofttimes it hath cast him into the fire, and into the waters, to destroy him:" (Mark 9:22).

In verses 7-10, John describes these other-worldly creatures. Some have suggested that this was John's first-century description of a modern helicopter. However, the scripture states that an angel came from Heaven with a key and unlocked the bottomless pit. The angel did not unlock the hanger for a helicopter fleet.

> **Revelation 9:7** And the shapes of the locusts were like unto horses prepared unto battle; and on their heads were as it were crowns like gold, and their faces were as the faces of men.

The locust-scorpions look like "horses prepared unto battle." They wear "crowns like gold," and their facial appearances are, "as the faces of men."

> **Revelation 9:8-9** And they had hair as the hair of women, and their teeth were as the teeth of lions. ⁹ And they had breastplates, as it were breastplates of iron; and the sound of their wings was as the sound of chariots of many horses running to battle.

John said he saw "hair as the hair of women," and that they had ravenous "teeth of lions." They also wear "breastplates of iron," and fly on wings that thunder "as the sound of chariots of many horses." God showed the prophet Joel a very similar prophetic image, "Like **the noise of chariots** on the tops of mountains shall they leap, like the noise of a flame of fire that devoureth the stubble, as a strong people **set in battle array**" (Joel 2:5).

> **Revelation 9:10** And they had tails like unto scorpions, and there were stings in their tails: and their power was to hurt men five months.

The weapon of these demonic locusts will be their "tails like unto scorpions." These creatures will sting those without God's seal, causing almost half a year of incredible pain. Joel's prophecy gives a similar description, "Before their face the people **shall be much pained**: all faces shall gather blackness" (Joel 2:6).

> **Revelation 9:11** And they had a king over them, which is the angel of the bottomless pit, whose name in the Hebrew tongue is Abaddon, but in the Greek tongue hath his name Apollyon.

The fact that these monstrous creatures "had a king over them," also supports an interpretation that the locusts from the pit are demons ruled by a demonic general. The meaning of their king's Hebrew name, Abaddon, is "destroyer."

Some suggest that this king must be Satan. However, Satan will not be imprisoned in the bottomless pit until after the end of the great tribulation (Rev. 20:1-2). This demonic general is what Paul called "a ruler of darkness" (Eph. 6:12). Don't confuse this demon with the angel from verses 1 and 2 who was from Heaven bringing the key to unlock this dark abyss.

> **Revelation 9:12** One woe is past; and, behold, there come two woes more hereafter.

Verses 13 and 14 begin the second woe, the sixth trumpet judgment.

**Trump of Destroyers**

> **Revelation 9:13-14** And the sixth angel sounded, and I heard a voice from the four horns of the golden altar which is before God, [14] Saying to

the sixth angel which had the trumpet, Loose
the four angels which are bound in the great
river Euphrates.

The "four angels which are bound" are four fallen angels or
demons. Jude also mentioned fallen angels bound in darkness
until the final days. "And the angels which kept not their first
estate, but left their own habitation, he hath reserved in everlasting chains under darkness unto the judgment of the great
day" (Jude 1:6).

The location of their prison, "the great river Euphrates," has an
interesting historical background. McGee explains:

> The Garden of Eden was somewhere in this section.
> The sin of man began here. The first murder was com-
> mitted here. The first war was fought here. Here was
> where the Flood began and spread over the earth.
> Here is where the Tower of Babel was erected. To this
> area were brought the Israelites of the Babylonian
> captivity.[38]

Chapter 18 identifies the center of the Antichrist's empire is a new
Babylon. The area of the Euphrates River has a significant history
and is a strategic location in end-times prophecy.

> **Revelation 9:15** And the four angels were
> loosed, which were prepared for an hour, and
> a day, and a month, and a year, for to slay the
> third part of men.

These fallen angels are loosed at God's appointed time, on a specific "hour, and a day, and a month..." Osborne commented about
God's sovereignty and Satan's lack of autonomy:

> This parallels 13:7, in which the beast 'is given authority
> to make war against the saints.' This is part of an

important theme in this book. Even the demonic forces can do nothing, unless God allows it! Many have the mistaken opinion that Satan has autonomy from God and can do whatever he wishes. That could not be further from the truth. Satan is powerless and has already lost at the cross (see 5:6).[39]

> **Revelation 9:16** And the number of the army of the horsemen were two hundred thousand thousand: and I heard the number of them.

The troops in this demonic army will number 200 million! In 2020, the total estimated military forces of all the countries in the world was over 21 million worldwide. This demonic force will be ten times the current size of the world's combined armed forces.

> **Revelation 9:17** And thus I saw the horses in the vision, and them that sat on them, having breastplates of fire, and of jacinth, and brimstone: and the heads of the horses were as the heads of lions; and out of their mouths issued fire and smoke and brimstone.

These demonic troops will ride horses that could star in the worst horror movie. The warhorses John saw were unlike anything in this world, with "heads of lions," breathing out "fire and smoke and brimstone."

Joel also prophesied of this coming judgment.

> A great people and a strong; there hath not been ever the like, neither shall be any more after it, even to the years of many generations. ³ A **fire devoureth before them**; and behind them a flame burneth: the land is as the garden of Eden before them, and behind them a desolate wilderness; yea, and nothing shall escape them. ⁴ The appearance of them is **as the**

**appearance of horses**; and as horsemen, so shall they run (Joel 2:2-4).

> **Revelation 9:18** By these three was the third part of men killed, by the fire, and by the smoke, and by the brimstone, which issued out of their mouths.

The fire, smoke, and brimstone will cause the deaths of another one-third of Earth's remaining population. Revelation 6 prophesied the deaths of twenty-five percent of the world (Rev. 6:7-8). The death of another one-third of the survivors will mean the loss of another 1.89 billion lives! No world war even comes close to this catastrophic loss of life. **Over half of the world's population** will be dead by the end of the sixth trumpet judgment.

The survivors of all these judgments will fear the eventual destruction of all humanity. Jesus warned, "And except those days should be shortened, there should no flesh be saved:" (Matt. 24:22).

> **Revelation 9:19** For their power is in their mouth, and in their tails: for their tails were like unto serpents, and had heads, and with them they do hurt.

Tozer notes that the source of these judgments will be undeniable:

> I am convinced that when the living Lord of Creation, the Almighty God, begins to bring this rebel world back into the divine orbit, there will be an invasion from the world above as well as from the world below. Once the trumpets have sounded, sinful men and women will have no recourse. Neither will they have questions as to the origin of the judgment. There will be no need for a governmental inquiry or investigation. All will know that they have come to the time of God's judgment throughout the world.[40]

After five months of severe torture, followed by the death of millions, most would expect the survivors to fall on their knees before Almighty God and repent. However, verses 20 and 21 describe their rebellious response.

> **Revelation 9:20-21** And the rest of the men which were not killed by these plagues yet repented not of the works of their hands, that they should not worship devils, and idols of gold, and silver, and brass, and stone, and of wood: which neither can see, nor hear, nor walk: [21] Neither repented they of their murders, nor of their sorceries, nor of their fornication, nor of their thefts.

Throughout these many phases of divine judgment, God demonstrates again and again that he has provided the unsaved every opportunity to repent and accept Jesus Christ, yet many will reject him.

Under the Antichrist, unbelievers will choose to reject God for the worship of devils and idolatrous statues, "the work of their hands." As pharaoh hardened his heart during the Exodus (1 Sam. 6:6), so the tribulation world will harden their hearts against God's wrath and continue turn to "idols of gold and silver." With Christianity out of the picture after the Rapture, idolatry will fill the spiritual gap and become the one-world religion.

Ironside commented:

> Both here, and later in this same book, we find that the heaviest judgments of God, falling on guilty men, do not soften the stony, rebellious hearts; but that rather men become hardened in their sins and are more blasphemous and God-defiant when judgment is poured out upon them than before.[41]

These closing verses of chapter 9 summarize the evil that will become commonplace during the great tribulation period. This chart shows that America is already on the same dangerous path.

| COMMON SINS DURING THE TRIBULATION | CURRENT SINS IN AMERICA |
|---|---|
| IDOLATRY "idols of gold, and silver" | In America there are approximately 450 Hindu Shrines, 25 Jain Shrines, and over 350 Buddhist Temples where idolatry is practiced. |
| MURDER "Neither repented they of their murders" | In America, almost 20,000 annually are murdered, not counting legal abortions, making the United States among the top five in the world. |
| SORCERY "nor of their sorceries": | In America there are approximately 340,000 practicing Wicca, and 1.5 million practicing Witchcraft or sorcery. In the original Greek, *pharmakon* also included magic potions, which today has become the drug culture in modern society. The use and abuse of drugs in America continues to climb. In 2018, over 53 million were trapped in this destructive habit. |
| FORNICATION "nor of their fornication" | In America, approximately 40 million visit pornography sites, 65 million have incurable sexually transmitted diseases with 15 million new cases are reported annually, and over 18,000 fall victim to sex trafficking each year. |
| THEFT "nor of their thefts" | In America, over 1.1 million vehicles are stolen per year and approximately $25 Billion per year is lost by retailers to shoplifting. |

Lessons from Chapter 9:

- **During the great tribulation, man will reject the true God and turn to worship false gods of their own making – idolatry.**

# CHAPTER 9 OUTLINE

VI. Seal of Doom (continued)

E. Trump of Demons 1-12

F. Trump of Destroyers 13-21

## CHAPTER 10

# A SERVANT'S COMMISSION

CHAPTER 10 IS ANOTHER TEXTUAL INTER-lude between the sixth and seventh trumpet judgments (Rev. 10-11). This parenthetical material will provide background details about the upcoming judgments. The time frame for these events is toward the end of the seven years of great tribulation.

> **Revelation 10:1** And I saw another mighty angel come down from heaven, clothed with a cloud: and a rainbow was upon his head, and his face was as it were the sun, and his feet as pillars of fire:

### A Solemn Proclamation

Some suggest that the description of "another mighty angel" must refer to Jesus. However, this **cannot be Jesus** for three reasons:

- Because the original word translated "another" indicates **another of the same kind**. This angel is similar to other great or mighty angels in Revelation (cf. Rev. 18:1).

- John saw this angel coming "down from heaven." Jesus returns to the earth for his second coming, leading the armies of Heaven into the Battle of Armageddon (Rev. 19:11).

- **This angel will swear by the Creator (verses 5-6).** If this is Jesus, he would be swearing by himself (cf. Heb. 6:13).

This angel will be "clothed with a cloud: and a rainbow" and "his face was as it were the sun." The angel in chapter 18, has a similar appearance, "the earth was lightened with his glory." Like these angels, Moses' face glowed when he came down from God's presence on Mount Sinai (Ex. 34:29-30). The face of this angel will shine like the sun because he comes from the glory of God's heavenly throne room.

> **Revelation 10:2** And he had in his hand a little book open: and he set his right foot upon the sea, and his left foot on the earth,

The mighty angel will carry "a little book open." A record of the book's contents is coming up.

In John's day, when one "set his right foot" upon something, it indicated authority over that which was under their foot. Judgments on the earth and sea are pronounced by this mighty angel.

> **Revelation 10:3** And cried with a loud voice, as when a lion roareth: and when he had cried, seven thunders uttered their voices.

Throughout Revelation, when thunder or lightning occurs, it usually indicates wrath or judgment. Ladd commented on the seven thunders:

> The only hint we have as to the message of the seven thunders is to be found in the fact that in all other passages in the Revelation where thunders occur, they form a premonition of coming judgments of divine wrath (8:5; 11:19; 16:18). This fits the present context, for the angel announces that the consummation of the divine judgments is about to take place.[42]

The "seven thunders" are a prophetic announcement of seven more judgments.

> **Revelation 10:4** And when the seven thunders had uttered their voices, I was about to write: and I heard a voice from heaven saying unto me, Seal up those things which the seven thunders uttered, and write them not.

John heard these prophecies and was about to record them. Like the prophet Daniel (Dan. 12:4), the Lord said, "Seal up those things... write them not."

McGee commented about many of the speculations regarding what the seven thunders may represent:

> There are wild speculators who have made ridiculous guesses. Vitringa interpreted the seven thunders as the seven Crusades. Danbuz made them the seven nations which received the Reformation. Elliot believed them to be the pope's bull against Luther. Several of the cults have presumed to reveal the things which were uttered.[43]

The contents of the seven thunders remain hidden to this day for reasons we may not learn until Jesus returns.

> **Revelation 10:5-6** And the angel which I saw stand upon the sea and upon the earth lifted up his hand to heaven, [6] And sware by him that liveth for ever and ever, who created heaven, and the things that therein are, and the earth, and the things that therein are, and the sea, and the things which are therein, that there should be time no longer:

The source of the angel's authority is from "him that liveth for ever and ever," the creator of Heaven and Earth. His proclamation "there should be time no longer," indicates that time has run out. When the seventh trumpet sounds, without further delay, the final judgments will begin.

Peter reminds us, "The Lord is not slack concerning his promise, as some men count slackness; but is longsuffering to us-ward, not willing that any should perish, but that all should come to repentance" (2 Pet. 3:9). It has never been God's desire for anyone to perish and spend eternity in the Lake of Fire. It has always been God's loving plan to give every individual the opportunity to repent, trust in Jesus, and spend eternity with him. However, as the last trumpet judgment sounds, sinful man will be **out of time**.

> **Revelation 10:7** But in the days of the voice of the seventh angel, when he shall begin to sound, the mystery of God should be finished, as he hath declared to his servants the prophets.

Verse 7 indicates that "the mystery of God" will be finished or complete. His divine plan for this world, His chosen people, and the coming kingdom will all "be finished." MacArthur comments on God's plan:

> To believers living at that time in a world overrun by demons, murder, sexual immorality, drug abuse, thefts, and unparalleled natural disasters, the realization that God's glorious plan is on schedule, the promised kingdom is near, when 'the earth will be filled with the knowledge of the glory of the Lord as the waters cover the sea' (Hab. 2:14), will bring great comfort and hope in the midst of judgment.[44]

**A Servant's Commission**

> **Revelation 10:8-9** And the voice which I heard from heaven spake unto me again, and said, Go and take the little book which is open in the hand

> of the angel which standeth upon the sea and
> upon the earth. [9] And I went unto the angel,
> and said unto him, Give me the little book. And
> he said unto me, Take it, and eat it up; and it shall
> make thy belly bitter, but it shall be in thy mouth
> sweet as honey.

The angel commands John to devour the contents of the little book. He was warned, "it shall make thy belly bitter." Jeremiah (Jer. 15) and Ezekiel (Ezek. 2) both had similar experiences. God commanded these Old Testament prophets to consume his prophetic word. The psalmist wrote, "How sweet are thy words unto my taste! yea, sweeter than honey to my mouth" (Ps. 119:103). John explains why this book would taste so sweet but become bitter.

> **Revelation 10:10-11** And I took the little book
> out of the angel's hand, and ate it up; and it was in
> my mouth sweet as honey: and as soon as I had
> eaten it, my belly was bitter. [11] And he said unto
> me, Thou must prophesy again before many peoples, and nations, and tongues, and kings.

Revelation provides "sweet as honey" prophecies of a bright future in Christ's kingdom. Verses 10 and 11 also tell us that this little book contains bitter warnings about severe judgments to come. John was being **re-commissioned** to prophesy the final trumpet judgment.

As believers, we have the privilege to consume, digest, and absorb God's Word. As we do, it becomes part of our heart, mind, and soul. It is sweet as honey in its encouraging and uplifting promises. The psalmist praised the sweetness of God's Word, "More to be desired are they than gold, yea, than much fine gold: sweeter also than honey and the honeycomb" (Ps. 19:10).

The judgments of God's Word on an ungodly, Christ-rejecting world are bitter as gall. Wiersbe explained:

God will not thrust His Word into our mouths and force us to receive it. He hands it to us, and we must take it. Nor can He change the effects the word will have in our lives: There will be both sorrow and joy, bitterness and sweetness. God's Word contains sweet promises and assurances, but it also contains bitter warnings and prophecies of judgment.[45]

Eating the book acknowledged John's **acceptance of God's commission** to deliver the final prophecies to "many peoples, and nations, and tongues, and kings."

Lessons from Chapter 10:

- **It has never been God's desire to see anyone perish and be cast into the Lake of Fire. It has always been God's loving plan to give every individual every opportunity to repent.**

- **God's Word is sweet as honey in its encouraging, uplifting promises. God's Word is also bitter as gall in its judgments on an ungodly Christ-rejecting world.**

## CHAPTER 10 OUTLINE

1. The Word

   A.  A Solemn Proclamation 1-7

   B.  A Servant's Commission 8-11

## CHAPTER 11

# THE TWO WITNESSES

**THE MESSAGE OF THE WITNESSES**

> **Revelation 11:1** And there was given me a reed like unto a rod: and the angel stood, saying, Rise, and measure the temple of God, and the altar, and them that worship therein.

To understand this command to "MEA-sure the temple" one must consider Old Testament prophetic background. God also gave Ezekiel (Ezek. 40, 45) and Zechariah (Zech. 2) the same directive.

God's command to measure something has a poignant Biblical meaning:

- The term was used of Moab, "he smote Moab, and measured them with a line..." (2 Sam. 8:2).

- Solomon used this term regarding Jerusalem, "The LORD hath purposed to destroy the wall of the daughter of Zion: he hath stretched out a line..." (Lam. 2:8).

The command to **measure** is a **symbolic act indicating God's** authority over that which is measured. It is as if there was a dispute over a property and they re-measured the property lines. The temple, the altar, and the worshippers were all to be re-measured. All were under God's jurisdiction.

John wrote Revelation late in the first century. The Temple was destroyed by the Romans in AD 70. The Temple in Jerusalem lay in total ruins for over 25 years before John wrote Revelation. Verse 1 commands John to measure a temple that did not exist, or to measure a future temple, one rebuilt at some point prior. Prophecies in Daniel 9 (Dan. 9:24-27), 2 Thessalonians (2 Thess. 2:2-4), and here in Revelation all indicate that there will be another Holy Temple in Jerusalem prior to the seven-year reign of the Antichrist.

The al-Aqsa Mosque and the Dome of the Rock were built in AD 691 by an Arab caliph. They were built on part of the original grounds of the Temple. Muslims claim that these buildings are their third most sacred site, where Mohammed ascended to Heaven.

Many Jews anticipate the rebuilding of the Temple in Jerusalem. Due to the preparations already completed, they estimate that a temple could be rebuilt in about two years.

> **Revelation 11:2** But the court which is without the temple leave out, and measure it not; for it is given unto the Gentiles: and the holy city shall they tread under foot forty and two months.

Jerusalem is considered "the holy city:"

- by Christians because Jesus died there
- by Jews because the Holy Temple was located there
- by Muslims because Muhammad ascended to Heaven from there

In his warning in Matthew 24, Jesus quoted a prophecy from Daniel 9, "When ye therefore shall see the abomination of desolation, spoken of by Daniel the prophet, stand in the holy place,..." (Matt. 24:15). Chapter 13 explains this in greater detail.

The angel's mention of "forty and two months" or three and one-half years is the first reference in Revelation to the specific time-frame for any part of the tribulation. This time frame fits the end-times prophecy in Daniel 9 regarding the seventy weeks (Dan. 9:24-27), particularly verse 27, focusing on the tribulation period.

> **Revelation 11:3** And I will give power unto my two witnesses, and they shall prophesy a thousand two hundred and threescore days, clothed in sackcloth.

This prophecy regarding "a thousand two hundred and threescore days" also verifies three and one-half years. The Jewish calendar during the Bible days used twelve thirty-day months. The "two witnesses" will preach the first half of the tribulation period, dressed "in sackcloth" or burlap, the garment of grief and repentance.

It is not possible to guess the identity of these two witnesses. Although many have offered possible candidates, the scripture does provide us that information. When God's Word does not provide details, it is either not for the readers to know or not important enough for God to reveal and preserve. Newell wrote, "Let it be at once observed, though it may not be pleasing, that the question is not who these witnesses are. If that had been important here, God would plainly have told us."[46]

> **Revelation 11:4** These are the two olive trees, and the two candlesticks standing before the God of the earth.

This verse indicates that the two witnesses will be a fulfillment of another Old Testament prophesy from the book of Zechariah:

And I answered again, and said unto him, What be these two olive branches which through the two golden pipes empty the golden oil out of themselves? [13] And he answered me and said, Knowest thou not what these be? And I said, No, my lord. [14] Then said he, These are **the two anointed ones**, that stand by the Lord of the whole earth (Zech. 4:12-14).

This prophecy originally referred to Zerubbabel, a post-exilic Jewish leader, and to Joshua, the high priest at that time (Zech. 3:1). These two chosen men helped reestablish Israel in the Promised Land after the seventy-year captivity, and they also **helped rebuild the Temple** (Zech. 4:9).

The olive oil and light from the "two candlesticks" represent the witnesses' prophetic ministry (Zech. 4:11). They will bring the light of truth to this world, lost in darkness under the Antichrist.

> **Revelation 11:5** And if any man will hurt them, fire proceedeth out of their mouth, and devoureth their enemies: and if any man will hurt them, he must in this manner be killed.

This text indicates that anyone attempting to "hurt them" will die as the fires of judgment are called down! Until their ministry is complete, these two witnesses will be protected by God. One can imagine how this will frustrate Satan and the Antichrist.

> **Revelation 11:6** These have power to shut heaven, that it rain not in the days of their prophecy: and have power over waters to turn them to blood, and to smite the earth with all plagues, as often as they will.

Like Moses in Egypt or Elijah in Israel, the two witnesses will call on God to send a drought, turn water into blood, and cause any other plagues. God will hear and answer them in his divine power.

## THE MARTYRDOM OF THE WITNESSES

> **Revelation 11:7** And when they shall have finished their testimony, the beast that ascendeth out of the bottomless pit shall make war against them, and shall overcome them, and kill them.

"The beast that ascendeth out of the bottomless pit" is later identified as the Antichrist (Rev. 13:1). Chapters 13 and 17 will teach much more about him.

The ministry of the two witnesses contributes to the salvation of the multitudes (Rev. 7:9-17). They will have power "to smite the earth with all plagues...." The unsaved will blame all the plagues and destruction on them and their God (Rev. 9:20, 16:9).

The beast or Antichrist will "make war against them...." War is a common theme of Revelation.

- Michael and the angels will fight against the dragon, Satan (Rev. 12:7,17).

- The Antichrist will make war with believers (Rev. 13:4,7).

- The Antichrist will lead the world's armies against Jesus at the Battle of Armageddon (Rev. 19:11,19).

Osborne comments about the last battle:

> However, the whole theme of the book is the futility of these acts of rebellion against God and his people. There is actually no final 'war,' only a last act of defiance made by an already defeated foe, and the death of the saints is their actual victory over Satan (12:11).[47]

> **Revelation 11:8** And their dead bodies shall lie in the street of the great city, which spiritually is

called Sodom and Egypt, where also our Lord
was crucified.

Sodom and Gomorrah refused to repent, and the fire and brimstone fell upon them (Gen. 19:14). The two witnesses are killed in
a city "spiritually is called as Sodom." The location is clearly identified as, "where our Lord was crucified." Under the Antichrist's rule,
**Jerusalem** will be transformed from a holy city to **an unholy city**.

> **Revelation 11:9** And they of the people and kin-
> dreds and tongues and nations shall see their
> dead bodies three days and an half, and shall not
> suffer their dead bodies to be put in graves.

Prophecy does not explain the purpose of leaving their bodies
unburied. Perhaps the prophets publicly predict their resurrection, forcing the international media to keep their cameras and cell
phones pointed at their bodies. The entire world will watch and wait.

> **Revelation 11:10** And they that dwell upon the
> earth shall rejoice over them, and make merry,
> and shall send gifts one to another; because
> these two prophets tormented them that dwelt
> on the earth.

The reaction of the Antichrist's kingdom is revealing. The death of
the two witnesses will trigger an international celebration. Wiersbe
commented about their rejoicing:

> No doubt the TV cameras in Jerusalem will transmit
> the scene to people around the world, and the new ana-
> lysts will discuss its significance. The earth-dwellers
> will rejoice at their enemies' removal and will celebrate
> a 'satanic Christmas' by sending gifts to one another.[48]

Imagine crowds of people joyfully walking by the unburied corpses of the two witnesses. They will stop to curse or spit upon them, and then proceed to celebrate the victory of the Antichrist.

> **Revelation 11:11** And after three days and an half the Spirit of life from God entered into them, and they stood upon their feet; and great fear fell upon them which saw them.

One can only imagine CNN, NBC, and CBS all forced to broadcast breaking news in Jerusalem: "After three days, the two witnesses stood upon their feet." They will live-stream their resurrection around the world.

> **Revelation 11:12** And they heard a great voice from heaven saying unto them, Come up hither. And they ascended up to heaven in a cloud; and their enemies beheld them.

## DOES REVELATION 11 SUPPORT A MID-TRIBULATION RAPTURE?

Some use this "**Come up hither**" to support a mid-tribulation rapture of the church. There are several problems with this theory.

- Zechariah 4 connects the two witnesses with **Judaism**. There is no connection with the New Testament church.

- Although the Church is mentioned seventeen times in the first three chapters of Revelation, the Church is not the focus of the remaining chapters. Many reinterpret passages with symbols or events and claim they represent the Church. However, there are no specific references to the church from chapters 4 through 21.

- The Church is told to "watch and be sober" for the day of the Lord's return (1 Thess. 5:6). It is not told to watch for the arrival of the Antichrist.

In this author's opinion, this passage does not support a mid-tribulation rapture theory.

> **Revelation 11:13** And the same hour was there a great earthquake, and the tenth part of the city fell, and in the earthquake were slain of men seven thousand: and the remnant were affrighted, and gave glory to the God of heaven.

Four great earthquakes are recorded in Revelation, including one in verse 19. Some experts suggest that one of the most significant fault lines on Earth is along the Syrian African Rift. The rift runs through the Dead Sea, the Sea of Galilee, and the Golan Heights. What a significant location in light of this context.

The "remnant were affrighted" after this quake and will have a change of heart, "gave glory to the God of heaven." Not all who suffer through the outpouring of God's wrath will refuse to repent.

> **Revelation 11:14** The second woe is past; and, behold, the third woe cometh quickly.

The second woe was the sixth trumpet judgment. The seventh and final trumpet judgment in verse 15 is the third woe.

## TRUMP OF DOOM

> **Revelation 11:15** And the seventh angel sounded; and there were great voices in heaven, saying, The kingdoms of this world are become the kingdoms of our Lord, and of his Christ; and he shall reign for ever and ever.

In chapter 10, John wrote, "But in the days of the voice of the seventh angel, when he shall begin to sound, the mystery of God should be finished..." (Rev. 10:7). With the sounding of this last trumpet, we have come to **the beginning of the end**. These final prophecies regard seven vials or bowls of wrath.

During his questioning by Pilate before the cross, Jesus said, "My kingdom is not of this world" (John 18:36). Osborne highlights the change in perspective:

> Now that dichotomy is ended, and the heavenly kingdom has replaced the earthly as the true reality. This is a major emphasis of apocalyptic thought, that the true reality is the heavenly rather than the earthly. The wonderful message here is that at the eschaton the heavenly kingdom will be the *only* reality![49]

> **Revelation 11:16-17** And the four and twenty elders, which sat before God on their seats, fell upon their faces, and worshipped God, [17] Saying, We give thee thanks, O Lord God Almighty, which art, and wast, and art to come; because thou hast taken to thee thy great power, and hast reigned.

Before the final trumpet sounds, the glorified elders declare before God, "thou hast taken to thee thy great power, and has reigned." Verse 18 describe the five-fold results of this declaration of God's reign. These five points also provide a general outline for chapters 12-20.

> **Revelation 11:18** And the nations were angry, and thy wrath is come, and the time of the dead, that they should be judged, and that thou shouldest give reward unto thy servants the prophets, and to the saints, and them that fear thy name,

small and great; and shouldest destroy them which destroy the earth.

# 5-FOLD REACTION TO THE DECLARATION OF GOD'S REIGN

- **The Wrath of the Nations** – "the nations were angry." Our God reigns! The two witnesses prophesied the coming judgments, and those judgments began. That which causes rejoicing in Heaven, will bring about anger and resentment on this Earth (Rev. 16:9).

- **The Wrath of God** – "thy wrath is come." Although being postponed for so long, time will finally run out, "thy wrath is come" (Rev. 16:1).

- **The Time of the Dead** – "and the time of the dead, that they should be judged." Final judgment is coming for those who died without Christ. They will stand before the one who holds the "keys of hell and of death" (Rev. 1:18) and will be judged (Rev. 20:12-15).

- **The Reward of the Servants** – "that thou shouldest give reward unto thy servants." This prophecy looks forward to rewarding "the prophets, and to the saints, and them that fear thy name." God keeps his word and will reward his servants (Rev. 20:4-6).

- **The Destruction of the Destroyer** – "and shouldest destroy them which destroy the earth." Judgment on the Antichrist and his followers will occur. This prophecy points to the bowls of wrath to come, ultimately ending in the Antichrist's judgment (Rev. 20:9-10).

> **Revelation 11:19** And the temple of God was opened in heaven, and there was seen in his temple the ark of his testament: and there were

lightnings, and voices, and thunderings, and an earthquake, and great hail.

John began this chapter measuring the Temple that the Antichrist will defile during the last half of the tribulation. He ends this chapter with a glimpse of "the Temple of God" in Heaven.

Moses made the entire tabernacle, altars, and the ark after the model of those in God's Temple in Heaven. Hebrews records:

> Who serve unto the example and shadow of heavenly things, as Moses was admonished of God when he was about to make the tabernacle: for, See, saith he, that thou make all things according to the pattern showed to thee in the mount (Heb. 8:5).

Before explaining the final judgments contained in the last trumpet, the Lord focuses on the Antichrist and his rise to power.

Lesson from Chapter 11:

- **That which causes rejoicing in the glory of Heaven, may bring about anger and resentment to those who have chosen to walk in darkness.**

## CHAPTER 11 OUTLINE

(Interlude – Continued from Chapter 10)

2. The Witnesses 11:1-14

A. The Message of the Witnesses 1-6

B. The Martyrdom of the Witnesses 7-13

G. TRUMP OF DOOM (7th TRUMPET) 11:15-19

## CHAPTER 12

# GREAT WONDER IN HEAVEN

CHAPTER 12 IS ANOTHER INTERLUDE OR
parenthesis, as some call it. The Lord stops the action to reveal
details behind much that has already occurred or will soon occur.
This information is vital to the reader's understanding of the events,
and provides insight into the key participants in those events.

Because of the imagery in chapters 12 and 13, many consider interpreting these chapters the most challenging in Revelation. The author has followed a few fundamental principles or guidelines for a correct interpretation of this prophetic material:

- God is the expert at all language and communication. In God's inspired Word, he said what he intended. The reader should interpret the meaning literally unless it is clearly symbolic (see 2 Tim. 3:16-17).

- When the text is metaphor or symbolism, the Lord often provides the correct interpretation within other scripture. If the immediate text does not provide the meaning, the primary source of interpretive material should be sought in other scripture passages (Rom. 15:4).

- We should not automatically interpret prophecy symbolically or as metaphor. Some choose symbolism to allow their interpretation to change the intended meaning of the text.

Their purpose is not to seek an accurate interpretation but to make it fit a specific theological perspective (see Prov. 30:5-6; 2 Pet. 1:20).

There are three main characters in this prophetic vision:

- The Woman (Rev. 12:1) who represents the Nation of Israel.
- The Red Dragon (Rev. 12:3) which represents Satan.
- The Child (Rev. 12:5) who represents Jesus.

> **Revelation 12:1** And there appeared a great wonder in heaven; a woman clothed with the sun, and the moon under her feet, and upon her head a crown of twelve stars:

## SIGN OF THE WOMAN (Part 1)

Who would this woman symbolically represent? Ironside noted the importance of this issue,

> I have learned to look upon this twelfth chapter as the crucial test in regard to correct prophetic outline. If the interpreters are wrong as to the woman and the man-child, it necessarily follows that they will be wrong as to many things connected with them.[50]

John describes the woman, "clothed with the sun... moon... and crown of twelve stars." Joseph's dream and his father's interpretation offers an obvious parallel:

> And he dreamed yet another dream, and told it his brethren, and said, Behold, I have dreamed a dream more; and, behold, the **sun and the moon and the eleven stars** made obeisance to me. [10] And he told it to his father, and to his brethren: and his father rebuked him, and said unto him, What is this dream that thou

hast dreamed? Shall I and thy mother and thy brethren indeed come to bow down ourselves to thee to the earth? [11] And his brethren envied him; but his father observed the saying (Gen. 37:9-11).

Joseph's father, Jacob, gave the interpretation of the meaning of Joseph's dream:

- The Sun represents Joseph's father, Jacob or Israel.

- The Moon represents Joseph and Benjamin's mother, Rachel.

- The eleven stars symbolize his brothers, the patriarchs of the Tribes of Israel. Joseph himself is the twelfth star here in Revelation's prophecy.

The sign of the woman matches Joseph's dream. Since the description is tied to another Old Testament vision, the reader has clear direction regarding the meaning of the woman. The woman is a representation of **the Nation of Israel**.

> **Revelation 12:2** And she being with child cried, travailing in birth, and pained to be delivered.

Verse 5 explains more about the identity of the sign of the child. Verses 3-4 describe the next sign.

## SIGN OF THE RED DRAGON

> **Revelation 12:3** And there appeared another wonder in heaven; and behold a great red dragon, having seven heads and ten horns, and seven crowns upon his heads.

Verse 9 explains the meaning of "a great red dragon" or serpent: "And the great dragon was cast out, that old serpent, called the Devil, and Satan..." The red dragon represents the Devil or Satan.

Compare the description, "seven heads and ten horns, and seven crowns," with chapter 13: "And saw a beast rise up out of the sea, having seven heads and ten horns, and upon his horns ten crowns, and upon his heads the name of blasphemy" (Rev. 13:1).

Daniel 7 gives us the background to this strange symbolism:

> After this I saw in the night visions, and behold a fourth **beast**, dreadful and terrible, and strong exceedingly; and it had great iron teeth: it devoured and brake in pieces, and stamped the residue with the feet of it: and it was diverse from all the beasts that were before it; and it had **ten horns** (Dan. 7:7).

Daniel continues with an explanation of what the beast represents and the meaning of the ten horns:

> Thus he said, The fourth beast shall be the fourth kingdom upon earth, which shall be diverse from all kingdoms, and shall devour the whole earth, and shall tread it down, and break it in pieces. <sup>24</sup> And **the ten horns out of this kingdom are ten kings that shall arise**: and **another shall rise after them**; and he shall be diverse from the first, and he shall subdue three kings (Dan. 7:23-24).

The fourth beast in Daniel's vision represents the rise of the Roman Empire. Rome also points to a type of coming kingdom in the last days. Chapter 13 explains more details regarding the fourth beast. The heads, horns, and crowns of the red dragon symbolize this evil creature's power and authority.

> **Revelation 12:4** And his tail drew the third part of the stars of heaven, and did cast them to the earth: and the dragon stood before the woman which was ready to be delivered, for to devour her child as soon as it was born.

Verse 9 describes Satan's fall and that of the fallen angels. "He was cast out into the earth, and his angels were cast out with him." These "stars of heaven" represent fallen angels or demons.

Isaiah 14 gives us Satan's previous identity before his fall occurred. "How art thou fallen from heaven, O **Lucifer**, son of the morning! how art thou cut down to the ground, which didst weaken the nations" (Isa. 14:12). Satan's name was Lucifer which means "morning star." Isaiah explains that evil pride caused his downfall:

> For thou hast said in thine heart, I will ascend into heaven, I will exalt my throne above the stars of God: I will sit also upon the mount of the congregation, in the sides of the north: ¹⁴ I will ascend above the heights of the clouds; **I will be like the most High**" (Isa. 14:13-14).

Satan also caused the fall of one-third of the angels from Heaven. They followed him due to his prideful desire for a throne above God's throne.

The red dragon determined "to devour her child as soon as it was delivered." At Jesus' birth, King Herod had all the babies in Bethlehem slaughtered to kill the newborn king (Matt. 2:16).

The **red dragon represents Satan**.

## SIGN OF THE CHILD

> **Revelation 12:5** And she brought forth a man child, who was to rule all nations with a rod of iron: and her child was caught up unto God, and to his throne.

The description of the "man child" leads us to a prophecy from Psalm 2:

I will declare the decree: the LORD hath said unto me, **Thou art my Son**; this day have I **begotten** thee. [8] Ask of me, and I shall give thee the heathen for thine inheritance, and the uttermost parts of the earth for thy possession. [9] Thou shalt break them with **a rod of iron**; thou shalt dash them in pieces like a potter's vessel (Ps. 2:7-9).

Revelation 19 records the fulfillment of this prophecy about Christ, **"He shall rule them with a rod of iron**: and he treadeth the winepress of the fierceness and wrath of Almighty God" (Rev. 19:15).

The vision showed the child "caught up unto God." Acts 1 records, "And when he had spoken these things, while they beheld, he was taken up; and a cloud received him out of their sight" (Acts 1:9). After His resurrection, Jesus was caught up to the right hand of God and "to His throne." This prophecy from Psalm 2 could only refer to Jesus Christ, the Son of God.

**The child represents Jesus Christ**.

**SIGN OF THE WOMAN (Part 2)**

> **Revelation 12:6** And the woman fled into the wilderness, where she hath a place prepared of God, that they should feed her there a thousand two hundred and threescore days.

This additional information clarifies the sign of the woman. There are several significant **misinterpretations**.

- **The Church** – As the bride of Christ, some suggest the twelve stars represent the apostles. There is no Biblical basis suggesting that the bride of Christ gives birth to a man-child who ascends to God's throne. The woman cannot represent the Church.

- **Mary the Immaculate** – A study of Catholic images of Mary reveals that they portray her with a crown of twelve stars, the Sun gleaming behind her, and her feet standing on the Moon. However, scripture does not connect Joseph's vision to Mary. There is no record that Mary "fled into the wilderness" for three and one-half years (Rev. 12:6).

- **Christian Science**. Mary Baker Eddy taught that the woman represents her, the child is a symbol of Christian Science, and that the red dragon represents the mortal mind which sought to destroy her religion.

Since the dragon is Satan, and the baby is Jesus, we can confirm that **the woman** represents **Israel** from whom Jesus was a descendant when he was born.

- Israel's persecution by the Antichrist is clear (Rev. 11:1-12; 12:13-17).

- Birth terms have been identified with Israel in prophecy (Isa. 54:4-5; Jer. 4:31). "Be in pain, and labour to bring forth, O daughter of Zion, like a woman in travail:" (Mic. 4:10).

- The Church did not give birth to the Messiah, but he was from a Jewish lineage, "Unto **us** a child is born..." (Isa. 9:6). Jesus was a direct descendant of Jacob, the father of the Jews (Rom. 9:4-5).

- The reference to the Sun, Moon, and stars, as shown in Genesis 37, portrays the Nation of Israel. Through Mary, Jesus descended from Abraham and King David (Luke 3:31,34).

In this prophetic vision, the woman "fled into the wilderness." In Matthew 24, Jesus warned of a time during the tribulation when the Jews will need to flee Jerusalem "into the mountains" (Matt. 24:16). They will be unable to flee to Egypt, Libya, or Ethiopia (see Dan. 11:43). These same countries will launch an unsuccessful battle against the Antichrist.

That leaves a route to the Southeast (Dan. 11:33, 41). About 20 miles past the Dead Sea, is a mountainous area where there is an excellent widened road and bridge today. Across that bridge and up a narrow entrance, the road leads through the most rugged and inaccessible mountains to Petra.

Psalm 60 mentions the same area in Edom. "Who will bring me into the strong city? who will lead me into Edom?" (Ps. 60:9). The Edomites carved beautiful temples into the mountainsides. They carved dwellings and businesses into the rock face. Petra's ancient city, called Sela is one probable shelter to which the Jews might flee during the great tribulation. Petra's entrance narrows to 50 ft. or less, and the walls rise 500-700 feet, making for easy defense. Petra has become an UN-protected site, and efforts are underway to restore the ancient water system. The UN has invested millions in park excavation and improvement. Tourist guides in Petra state that Petra's large city could easily hold up to 5 million people!

Notice "they will feed her there" for 1,260 days, or three and one-half Jewish years. Daniel 11 mentions three countries the Antichrist will not overthrow, "these shall escape out his hand, even Edom, and Moab, and the chief of the children of Ammon" (Dan. 11:33). Today these areas are all part of Jordan, one of the few neighbors on more friendly terms with Israel since a 1994 peace treaty.

> **Revelation 12:7-8** And there was war in heaven: Michael and his angels fought against the dragon; and the dragon fought and his angels, [8] And prevailed not; neither was their place found any more in heaven.

When could this war between the archangel Michael and Satan occur? Some suggest the event happened at some time in the past. Verse 12 indicates that after losing heavenly access, the Devil will know "he hath but a short time." The author suggests that the short time following the war, and references in this chapter to a three-and one-half-year period, indicates these events occur around the mid-point of the seven-year tribulation.

Daniel prophesied this time of trouble for Israel:

> And at that time shall **Michael** stand up, the great prince which standeth for the children of thy people: and there shall be a time of trouble, such as never was since there was a nation even to that same time: and at that time thy people shall be delivered, every one that shall be found written in the book. [4] But thou, O Daniel, shut up the words, and seal the book, even to the time of the end: many shall run to and fro, and knowledge shall be increased (Dan. 12:1, 4).

Every word of God is as sure and unchanging as God is. Although Satan may face Michael and the heavenly angels in a future battle, this prophecy proclaims that **the Devil will not win**. Verse 8 proclaims, he "prevailed not."

> **Revelation 12:9** And the great dragon was cast out, that old serpent, called the Devil, and Satan, which deceiveth the whole world: he was cast out into the earth, and his angels were cast out with him.

Satan, "that old serpent" from Eden's garden (Gen. 3:1), will lose his access to Heaven. Verse 12 prophesies the result of his expulsion from Heaven.

> **Revelation 12:10** And I heard a loud voice saying in heaven, Now is come salvation, and strength, and the kingdom of our God, and the power of his Christ: for the accuser of our brethren is cast down, which accused them before our God day and night.

The Lord calls Satan "the accuser of our brethren," the fourth descriptive term for Satan in this chapter:

- The Dragon (Rev. 12:3) or "old serpent" (Gen. 3)

- The Devil (Rev. 12:9)

- Satan (Rev. 12:9), which means our enemy

- The Accuser (Rev. 12:10)

Before his defeat to Michael, Satan appeared "before our God day and night" and brought accusations against believers. As God's children, we should ask ourselves if our attitudes or actions might be providing Satan with evidence to use against us. We demonstrate our love for the Lord in our obedience and holy living.

> **Revelation 12:11** And they overcame him by the blood of the Lamb, and by the word of their testimony; and they loved not their lives unto the death.

Notice three ways these tribulation saints will overcome Satan:

- "By the blood of the Lamb" – All victory over Satan comes through Christ alone (1 Cor. 15:57). Believers cannot overcome the Accuser. The shed blood of Christ covers our sins (Rev. 1:5). Our victory over Satan's darts and temptations is not by our efforts but by Christ's sacrifice (Eph. 6:10).

- "By the word of their testimony" – Satan is overcome by their faithful witness. Regardless of the spiritual darkness of the time, believers of all ages need to be faithful witnesses.

- "They loved not their lives" – Most of these believers will choose martyrdom for their faith. These believer's deaths may seem like a defeat for the cause of Christ. Nevertheless, their sacrifice for the sake of the Gospel will overcome Satan (Rev. 2:10).

> **Revelation 12:12** Therefore rejoice, ye heavens, and ye that dwell in them. Woe to the inhabiters of the earth and of the sea! for the devil is come down unto you, having great wrath, because he knoweth that he hath but a short time.

Three "woes" were prophesied (Rev. 8:13):

- The fifth trumpet judgment (Rev. 9:12)

- The sixth trumpet judgment (Rev. 11:14)

- The seventh trumpet judgment (Rev. 12:12)

This final woe begins in verse 12 and will continue through the entire second half of the tribulation.

Satan is forced down to the Earth with all the fallen angels in furious defeat.

> **Revelation 12:13** And when the dragon saw that he was cast unto the earth, he persecuted the woman which brought forth the man child.

Violently angry over his expulsion from Heaven, Satan will attack the woman who represents the surviving tribulation Jews. The prophet Jeremiah called these days "the time of Jacob's trouble" (Jer. 30:7). In answer to the disciple's question about the end times, Jesus warned about the coming days of severe persecution. "For then shall be great tribulation, such as was not since the beginning of the world to this time, no, nor ever shall be" (Matt. 24:21). The Antichrist will violate his initial peace treaty and turn the wrath of his demonic master upon the Jews.

> **Revelation 12:14** And to the woman were given two wings of a great eagle, that she might fly into the wilderness, into her place, where she is

nourished for a time, and times, and half a time,
from the face of the serpent.

Some suggest "a great eagle" may refer to the United States. However, this is mostly wishful thinking without any clear Biblical basis. In the book of Exodus, the eagle symbolized God's deliverance of his people from bondage. "Ye have seen what I did unto the Egyptians, and how I bare you on eagles' wings, and brought you unto myself" (Exod. 19:4). The eagle is a figure of speech commonly indicating swift deliverance.

In this verse, we find a rather poetic way to describe three and one-half years of tribulation: a time (1 +), and times (2 +), and half a time (½). The remnant of the surviving Jews will be hidden in the wilderness where God protects them during the great tribulation.

> **Revelation 12:15** And the serpent cast out of his mouth water as a flood after the woman, that he might cause her to be carried away of the flood.

Scripture indicates that Satan can cause natural disasters. He destroyed Job's sheep and his shepherds by fire (Job 1:16) and killed his children in a house destroyed by a tornado (Job 1:19). In this verse, Satan could easily cause a flood of water in his attempt to destroy Israel's remnant.

> **Revelation 12:16** And the earth helped the woman, and the earth opened her mouth, and swallowed up the flood which the dragon cast out of his mouth.

The Old Testament records that the Lord caused the earth to open before, during a rebellion in Moses' day. "And the earth opened her mouth, and swallowed them up, and their houses, and all the men that appertained unto Korah, and all their goods" (Num. 16:32). Here in this verse, we see the mighty power of God at work providing divine protection.

> **Revelation 12:17** And the dragon was wroth with
> the woman, and went to make war with the rem-
> nant of her seed, which keep the commandments
> of God, and have the testimony of Jesus Christ.

Not all the believing Jews will make it to safety from this attack on Israel. Some will stay behind but will not find protection. This "remnant of her seed" will include the 144,000 sealed by God and entrusted with the "testimony of Jesus Christ." Chapter 14 mentions them again.

Zechariah also prophesied the protection of a remnant of the Jews:

> And it shall come to pass, that in all the land, saith
> the LORD, two parts therein shall be cut off and die;
> but the third shall be left therein. ⁹ And I will bring
> the third part through the fire, and will refine them as
> silver is refined, and will try them as gold is tried: they
> shall call on my name, and I will hear them: I will say,
> It is my people: and they shall say, The LORD is my
> God. (Zech. 13:8-9).

Chapter 12 provides an overview of the rise of the Antichrist. Chapter 13 explains the vivid details.

Lessons from Chapter 12:

- **God is the expert communicator. In God's Word, he said what he intended. The reader should take his meaning literally unless it is clearly symbolic. When the text is metaphorical or symbolic, the reader should use other scripture to explain the meaning.**

- **Just because the text is Bible prophecy, it should not automatically be interpreted symbolically, forcing it to fit a preferred theology!**

# CHAPTER 12 OUTLINE

1. Wonder in Heaven 1-6
2. War in Heaven 7-11
3. Wilderness Help 12-17

# CHAPTER 13

# THE MARK OF THE BEAST

C HAPTER 13 CONTAINS SOME OF THE MOST significant prophecies about the tribulation period contained in the entire Bible. This chapter focuses on the Antichrist. The term "antichrist" comes from John's first letter, "it is the last time: and as ye have heard that **antichrist** shall come" (1 Jo. 2:18).

The descriptions in this chapter includes two beasts which are both symbolic:

- **The first beast** from the sea represents the Antichrist (Rev. 13:1-10).

- **The second beast** from the Earth represents the False Prophet (Rev. 13:11-18).

> **Revelation 13:1** And I stood upon the sand of the sea, and saw a beast rise up out of the sea, having seven heads and ten horns, and upon his horns ten crowns, and upon his heads the name of blasphemy.

## SIGN OF THE BEAST FROM THE SEA

John was imprisoned on the Isle of Patmos. When John "stood upon the sand of the sea," the Aegean Sea was closest to him. The Aegean is part of the Mediterranean Sea. "Out of the sea" suggests that the Antichrist and his kingdom will come from the Mediterranean area.

The beast John saw has "seven heads," like the red dragon which represents Satan (Rev. 12:3). We will find another connection with the dragon in verse 2.

The symbolism of the beast is clarified in chapter 17:

- The "seven heads" John saw symbolize seven hills indicating a location (Rome), as well as seven kings. The Antichrist originally comes from these seven (Rev. 17:10-11).

- The "ten horns" represent ten rulers forming a coalition under the Antichrist (Rev. 17:12-13).

The structure for this empire may already be in existence. Considering the rather complex depiction of the beast, keep in mind that it not only represents **a real man who will be king**, but **also his kingdom**. Some symbols refer to the Antichrist, while others refer to his kingdom.

> **Revelation 13:2** And the beast which I saw was like unto a leopard, and his feet were as the feet of a bear, and his mouth as the mouth of a lion: and the dragon gave him his power, and his seat, and great authority.

Daniel's prophecy, recorded in chapter 7, looked forward from the empire of Babylon to the Roman Empire. In John's day, his vision began with the present and looked back to past empires. John's list starts with Rome, the final empire from Daniel's prophecy, and works backward:

The first was like **a lion**, and had eagle's wings: I beheld till the wings thereof were plucked, and it was lifted up from the earth, and made stand upon the feet as a man, and a man's heart was given to it. ⁵ And behold another beast, a second, like to **a bear**, and it raised up itself on one side, and it had three ribs in the mouth of it between the teeth of it: and they said thus unto it, Arise, devour much flesh. ⁶ After this I beheld, and lo another, like **a leopard**, which had upon the back of it four wings of a fowl; the beast had also four heads; and dominion was given to it (Dan. 7:4-6).

The third beast in Daniel's dream is a winged Leopard representing the Greek Empire under Alexander the Great (Dan. 7:6). The second beast is a bear representing the Medo-Persian Empire (Dan. 7:5). The Babylonian Empire under Nebuchadnezzar is the first beast (Dan. 7:4).

Here in Revelation, one beast represents all three of these previous world empires. Satan will establish a one world empire under the Antichrist.

**Revelation 13:2-3** And the beast which I saw was like unto a leopard, and his feet were as the feet of a bear, and his mouth as the mouth of a lion: and the dragon gave him his power, and his seat, and great authority. ³ And I saw one of his heads as it were wounded to death; and his deadly wound was healed: and all the world wondered after the beast.

The Antichrist will be "wounded to death" by a sword (Rev. 13:14). The beast receives a fatal wound but then is "healed." Verse 14 gives some additional details. Satan uses this pseudo-miracle to cause the tribulation world to worship the Antichrist as their risen Messiah.

**Revelation 13:4** And they worshipped the dragon which gave power unto the beast: and they

worshipped the beast, saying, Who is like unto the
beast? who is able to make war with him?

Verse 8 explains, "all that dwell upon the earth shall worship him."
This one-world religion will require the World to bow the knee and
worship "the dragon." **Satan worship** will be mandatory throughout
the second half of the Antichrist's brief rule.

> **Revelation 13:5** And there was given unto him
> a mouth speaking great things and blasphemies;
> and power was given unto him to continue forty
> and two months.

Daniel also saw these dark details about the Antichrist in his prophetic vision: "In this horn were eyes like the eyes of man, and a
mouth speaking great things" (Dan. 7:8). "And he shall speak great
words **against the most High**..." (Dan. 7:25). This false Christ will
be a great orator, brilliant, and mesmerizing to the crowds. But his
message will be blasphemy against the one true God.

> **Revelation 13:6** And he opened his mouth in blas-
> phemy against God, to blaspheme his name, and
> his tabernacle, and them that dwell in heaven.

Blasphemy is a common feature of the daily addresses heard on the
airways during the Antichrist's reign. The basic definition of blasphemy in Scripture is calling yourself God (Jo. 10:33). Notice in this
verse that the Antichrist directs his evil speaking against three things:

- Against God's Name
- Against God's Temple
- Against God's People

Satan's human representative during the seven years of tribulation
will be anti-God, anti-Christian, and anti-Semitic. The Antichrist
opposes anything that has to do with Jesus or the salvation of man

from his sin. This cancel-culture may sound eerily current with the growing prevalence of today's anti-Christian, anti-Jewish culture here in America.

> **Revelation 13:7** And it was given unto him to make war with the saints, and to overcome them: and power was given him over all kindreds, and tongues, and nations.

The first seal pictures the Antichrist as a conquering king, "And I saw, and behold a white horse..." (Rev. 6:2).

For a short time, he will become the world ruler or emperor. During the temptation of Jesus in the wilderness, Satan originally offered him this same role:

> Again, the devil taketh him up into an exceeding high mountain, and showeth him all the kingdoms of the world, and the glory of them; [9] And saith unto him, **All these things will I give thee**, if thou wilt fall down and worship me (Matt. 4:8-9).

Although Jesus rejected Satan's offer, the Antichrist will rise to power, deceiving this fallen world into Satan worship.

> **Revelation 13:8** And all that dwell upon the earth shall worship him, whose names are not written in the book of life of the Lamb slain from the foundation of the world.

Ironside wrote:

> This coming one is the Grand Monarch of the New Humanity cult. He is the coming Imaum, or Mahdi, of the Mussulmans (Muslims), he is the long-expected last incarnation of Vishnu awaited by the Brahmins; the coming Montezuma of the Aztecs; the false Messiah

of the apostate Jews, the great Master of all sects of yogis; the Ultimate Man of the evolutionists; and the **Übermensch** of Nietzsche, the Hun philosopher whose ravings prepared the way for the world war.[51]

# THE BOOK OF LIFE IN REVELATION

There is only one reference to the Book of Life outside of Revelation (see Phil. 4:3). Consider Revelation's teaching about this sacred book:

- Those listed in the Book of Life will not worship the Antichrist (Rev. 13:8).

- The Lord recorded believer's names in the Book of Life at the beginning of creation (Rev. 17:8).

- The Lord uses the Book of Life at the final judgment (20:12).

- Those whose names do not appear the Book of Life will face a fiery eternity (20:15).

- Those named in the Book of Life enter the Lord's eternal kingdom (21:27).

It is sobering that this book **does not cause** unbeliever's coming judgment, but it **prophetically records it** (Rev. 17:8).

> **Revelation 13:9** If any man have an ear, let him hear.

This repeated phrase is missing something significant from previous usages. Jesus used it in all seven letters to the churches (Rev. 2:7, 11, 17, 29; 3:6, 13, 22). Each time in those letters, Jesus said, "If any man have an ear, let him hear what the Spirit saith unto the churches." In verse 9, there is an interesting omission of "**the churches**" compared to the phrase's previous usage.

> **Revelation 13:10** He that leadeth into captivity shall go into captivity: he that killeth with the sword must be killed with the sword. Here is the patience and the faith of the saints.

"The saints" will be led into captivity and killed "with the sword" during this time of spiritual darkness. Verse 10 prophesies that their persecutors will suffer the same consequences under the coming wrath of God, "must be killed with the sword." Even in this chapter about the world under Satanic rule, we see the continuing grace of God encouraging those whose faith will receive the ultimate test.

## THE SIGN OF THE BEAST FROM THE EARTH

> **Revelation 13:11** And I beheld another beast coming up out of the earth; and he had two horns like a lamb, and he spake as a dragon.

The word translated "another" indicates *another of a similar kind*. The Antichrist requires additional support to fulfill Satan's goals. In the vision, the beast does not appear to wear a crown. His power and authority are not political or military but is religious. He is a wolf in sheep's clothing (Matt. 7:15).

The beast "spake as a dragon." Like the serpent who whispered to Eve in the garden, through the False Prophet, Satan will speak guile to deceive man again.

> **Revelation 13:12** And he exerciseth all the power of the first beast before him, and causeth the earth and them which dwell therein to worship the first beast, whose deadly wound was healed.

This beast will be called "the false prophet" (Rev. 19:20). He completes a type of **fallen trinity**:

- Satan – the evil opposite of God the Father.

- The Antichrist – the mocking imitation of Jesus Christ.

- The False Prophet – the counterpart of the Holy Spirit.

The False Prophet promotes worldwide idolatry through mandatory worship of the Antichrist. So much for the separation of church and state, which Satan only supports when the church is primarily Christian.

> **Revelation 13:13** And he doeth great wonders, so that he maketh fire come down from heaven on the earth in the sight of men,

The False Prophet does "great wonders," including calling down fire. Paul foresaw his deception and chose another term to describe these wonders: "Even him, whose coming is after the working of Satan with all power and signs and **lying wonders**, [10] And with all deceivableness of unrighteousness in them that perish;" (2 Thess. 2:9-10). Signs and wonders are not reliable evidence we should trust, nor are they proof that God is responsible (2 Cor. 11:13-15).

In 1920, Dr. Ironside wrote what today still sounds quite contemporary:

> One of the signs of the times in our own days is the unhealthy craving for marvels and wonders, which is so prevalent in many quarters. It is a most dangerous condition of the mind, and Christians might well beware of anything of the kind. We are too near the end of the dispensation to expect divine miracles in any number; but Satanic signs and wonders will increase, as we draw nearer the end, and when the Antichrist himself appears, he will give men all the marvels for which they long – only to deceive them, and to lead them to accept his ungodly pretensions.[52]

Satan is a mighty cherubim, fallen and evil, capable of events that seem miraculous and supernatural here in our world. Many demons provide hidden help behind the scenes. Believers must see through his deception. We cannot trust signs and wonders to determine if a work is God's. We must rely solely upon God's unchanging Word. "For there shall arise false Christs, and false prophets, and shall shew great signs and wonders; insomuch that, if it were possible, they shall deceive the very elect" (Matt. 24:24).

The False Prophet uses what seems miraculous to persuade unbelievers to worship him. It will not stop there. Next will be a resurgence of idolatry.

> **Revelation 13:14** And deceiveth them that dwell on the earth by the means of those miracles which he had power to do in the sight of the beast; saying to them that dwell on the earth, that they should make an image to the beast, which had the wound by a sword, and did live.

There are several interpretations of the "wound by a sword, and did live:"

- Some suggest that a world leader will be **killed and resurrected** (i.e., Nero or Hitler). The text does not state that the Antichrist will die and rise from the dead, but that a deadly wound "was healed." Satan does not have the power to bring someone back from the dead (see John 5:21-29).

- Others interpret this symbolically and suggest this verse represents the death and resurrection of **an empire**. Due to Daniel's prophecies regarding coming kingdoms (see Dan. 7), the Roman Empire is considered a type of the Antichrist's kingdom.

- The author suggests interpreting "The wound by a sword" to mean that the Antichrist receives a deadly wound. That he "did live," indicates he claims to have risen from the dead.

McGee wrote:

> I believe the Beast is a man who will exhibit a coun-
> terfeit and imitation resurrection. This will be a great
> delusion, the big lie of the great tribulation period. We
> are told that God will give them over to believe the big
> lie (see 2 Thess. 2:11), and this is part of the big lie. They
> will not accept the resurrection of Christ, but they sure
> are going to fake the resurrection of Antichrist.[53]

We don't have enough information to be conclusive about the
Antichrist's pseudo miracle. The author leans toward that which
provides the most plain and simple meaning of the text: The
Antichrist will receive a fatal wound. His promoters and the False
Prophet will then claim that the Antichrist died and returned
from the dead.

Like the mandatory worship of the "image to the beast" in verse 14,
Daniel recorded that Nebuchadnezzar built an image and forced
everyone in his kingdom to bow or burn (Dan. 3).

> **Revelation 13:15** And he had power to give life
> unto the image of the beast, that the image of
> the beast should both speak, and cause that as
> many as would not worship the image of the
> beast should be killed.

The idol of the Antichrist will appear to come to life. The False
Prophet could bring this about through demonic activity or by
some other means of automation and deception.

There will be initial resistance to the Antichrist's claim to be a god,
causing some to refuse to worship his statue. The False Prophet
will institute a new international death sentence for those who
refuse to bow. Satan has never believed in freedom of speech or
religious freedom!

The next development in the Antichrist's kingdom will be universal identification.

## THE MARK OF THE BEAST

> **Revelation 13:16** And he causeth all, both small and great, rich and poor, free and bond, to receive a mark in their right hand, or in their foreheads:

The word "mark" indicates an etching, stamp, or brand. Other than the locations, we don't have a scriptural indication of what sort of mark it is.

> **Revelation 13:17** And that no man might buy or sell, save he that had the mark, or the name of the beast, or the number of his name.

Verse 17 introduces a third element of the Antichrist's kingdom: worldwide economic control. On an international scale, many pieces of the prophetic puzzle are already in place:

- The push of America's political leadership toward Globalism
- Internationalizing military forces
- Computerization of banking
- The Euro as an example of a common currency

Notice the 3 types of government-mandated identification that are required during the great tribulation:

- "The mark" of the beast (Rev. 14:9) – The text indicates that the mark is a brand or stamp, which could be a visible or invisible tattoo.
- "The name of the beast" – The 144,000 were also sealed in their foreheads with the name of God (Rev. 14:1).

- "The number of his name" – Verse 13 explains that meaning of the number.

> **Revelation 13:18** Here is wisdom. Let him that hath understanding count the number of the beast: for it is the number of a man; and his number is Six hundred threescore and six.

The Lord does not provide an actual name but emphasizes its number: **666**. John admonished, "count" or calculate "the number of the beast." In John's day, there was not a Greek alphabet and an additional set of Greek numbers. The ancient world used a single set of symbols for both, every letter had a numeric meaning.

The Lord is not asking that believers should guess the Antichrist's identity, although many have tried. Perhaps, after the Rapture, those who study the Bibles left behind will recognize who the Antichrist is when he rises to power. They will calculate the number of his name, realize the mark's meaning for buying and selling, and understand that this ruler must be the Antichrist.

The symbolism of the number **666** is "the number of a man." Dr. Akin notes:

> I think the number is more of a description than an identification. Six is the number of man. He was created on the sixth day. He is to work six days. In contrast, the number of perfection is seven, and the superlative of seven is 777...He, along with Satan and the false prophet, is a 666, a trinity of imperfection. Not now or ever will they be a 777![54]

Lessons from Chapter 13:

- **During his temptation in the wilderness, Satan offered the Antichrist's role to Jesus, if he would bow and worship him (Luke 4:5-8).**

- **It is sobering that the Book of Life does not cause unbeliever's judgment, but it prophetically records it.**

- **Signs and wonders are not always trustworthy proof that God is at work.**

I. THE BEAST FROM THE SEA 1-10

    A.  Wonder of the Beast 1-3

    B.  Worship of the Beast 4-6

    C.  War of the Beast 7-10

II. THE BEAST FROM THE EARTH 11-18

    A.  Miracles of the Beast 11-15

    B.  Mark of the Beast 16-18

## CHAPTER 14

# THE LAMB ON MOUNT ZION

CHAPTER 14 CONCLUDES THIS INTERME-
diate section which began in chapter 12.

> **Revelation 14:1** And I looked, and, lo, a Lamb
> stood on the mount Sion, and with him an hun-
> dred forty and four thousand, having his Father's
> name written in their foreheads.

Several names of Jesus appear in this chapter.

- The Lamb of God – mentioned here and two other times
  (Rev. 14:1, 4, 10)

- Jesus – referred to in verse 12

- The Son of Man – used in verse 14

Psalm 51 notes that the location of Mount Zion is Jerusalem (Psa.
51:18). The Lamb standing on Zion is Jesus. The 144,000 are from
Revelation 7, the sealed tribulation saints from the twelve tribes of
Israel. Since Jesus does not return to Earth until his second coming,
this prophetic vision must occur **after the Battle of Armageddon**.

> **Revelation 14:2** And I heard a voice from heaven,
> as the voice of many waters, and as the voice of

a great thunder: and I heard the voice of harpers harping with their harps:

In verse 1, John saw the Lamb and the saints on Earth. Now he hears a voice from Heaven. The booming voice is the Lord's, and others join him. Those who do not believe in musical instruments for worship might struggle with this reference to singing and harps. Osborne offers some background to the harp in the Bible, "The harp was a ten-or twelve-string lyre used often in temple worship (Psa. 33:2; 57:8). In the apocalypse, harps are mentioned in Rev. 5:8; 14:2; 15:2; and 18:22."[55]

> **Revelation 14:3** And they sung as it were a new song before the throne, and before the four beasts, and the elders: and no man could learn that song but the hundred and forty and four thousand, which were redeemed from the earth.

God and His harpers are giving music lessons to the 144,000, teaching them the song of the redeemed. The prophet Zephaniah wrote, "The LORD thy God in the midst of thee is mighty; he will save, he will rejoice over thee with joy; he will rest in his love, **he will joy over thee with singing**" (Zeph. 3:17) This may be the only reference to God singing!

Isaiah also prophesied about this event. "Therefore the redeemed of the LORD shall return, and come with singing unto Zion; and everlasting joy shall be upon their head: they shall obtain gladness and joy; and sorrow and mourning shall flee away" (Isa. 51:11). One day soon, the redeemed tribulation saints will sing a new song and fulfill Isaiah's prophecy!

> **Revelation 14:4** These are they which were not defiled with women; for they are virgins. These are they which follow the Lamb whithersoever he goeth. These were redeemed from among men, being the firstfruits unto God and to the Lamb.

Verses 4 and 5 reveal several identifying characteristics of the 144,000:

- They are undefiled & holy. During the extreme persecution of the tribulation days, these servants of the Lord give themselves wholly unto God, keep themselves undefiled, and choose not to marry.

- They are unswervingly obedient. Like the Nazarites of old, the 144,000 are totally dedicated to serving the Lord.

- They are "firstfruits unto God." According to Jewish law, the firstfruits of the harvest always belong to the Lord. Walvoord explained,

    The term 'firstfruits' seems to refer to the beginning of a great harvest—here to the beginning of the millennial kingdom. The 144,000 are the godly nucleus of Israel that is the token of the redemption of the nation and the glory of Israel that is to unfold in the kingdom.[56]

    **Revelation 14:5** And in their mouth was found no guile: for they are without fault before the throne of God.

- They are without deceit or hypocrisy. The 144,000 are the holy opposite of the unholy lies and deception perpetrated by the Antichrist and False Prophet. Unlike the tribulation world in which they will live, the 144,000 speak the truth.

- They are without fault. Living holy lives, without deceit, God finds no blame in them.

Throughout the darkest spiritual time in history, the godly attributes and characteristics of the 144,000 should challenge every believer to ask God to make us more like Jesus.

> **Revelation 14:6** And I saw another angel fly
> in the midst of heaven, having the everlasting
> gospel to preach unto them that dwell on the
> earth, and to every nation, and kindred, and
> tongue, and people,

This chapter introduces six angels, and chapter 15 writes about another seven. There is more recorded about angels in the book of Revelation than any other book of the Bible. The veil between our world and the unseen spiritual world will grow thin as we move toward these final events.

There is only one plan of salvation, and since the beginning, it has never changed! The "everlasting Gospel" continues to be offered and preached "to every nation, and kindred, and tongue, and people." It is not God's will that any should perish (2 Pet. 3:9), and unsaved man will one day stand before the Lord without excuse (Rom. 1:20).

Sadly, verse 6 records the **final reference to the Gospel** in all of God's Word. How sobering to realize that the last opportunity to repent and be saved will come during the tribulation period. We have no way to know how close we are to that day. Believers everywhere should fervently, boldly proclaim God's truth about salvation before it becomes too late.

> **Revelation 14:7** Saying with a loud voice, Fear
> God, and give glory to him; for the hour of his
> judgment is come: and worship him that made
> heaven, and earth, and the sea, and the fountains
> of waters.

Chapter 15 moves the chronology of Revelation forward toward the final outpouring of God's wrath. The angel admonishes all to **fear God** and **worship Him**. These two ingredients are already missing in most of society today. There is a sad lack of fear of the Lord and little true worship of the true God. In God's grace and mercy, America desperately needs to "Fear God, and give glory to him."

> **Revelation 14:8** And there followed another angel, saying, Babylon is fallen, is fallen, that great city, because she made all nations drink of the wine of the wrath of her fornication.

The angel in verse 8 gives us this first reference to a future Babylon. Chapters 17 and 18 provide a much fuller description and explanation. The Babylon of the Old Testament no longer exists. This prophecy indicates that another Babylon or type of Babylon will rise and fall during the Antichrist's reign.

> **Revelation 14:9** And the third angel followed them, saying with a loud voice, If any man worship the beast and his image, and receive his mark in his forehead, or in his hand,

The unsaved will bow and take the mark of the beast to avoid the wrath of the Antichrist. They will be unable to avoid God's wrath.

> **Revelation 14:10** The same shall drink of the wine of the wrath of God, which is poured out without mixture into the cup of his indignation; and he shall be tormented with fire and brimstone in the presence of the holy angels, and in the presence of the Lamb:

The final trumpet judgment pours out God's undiluted wrath. It is no longer mixed with grace or mercy. Ladd explained:

> In any case, God's wrath is not a human emotion; it is the settled reaction of his holiness to man's sinfulness and rebellion...Two of the main themes of the Revelation are the recalcitrance of men against God's

salvation, manifested in their subservience to the beast;
and the judgment of God which must fall upon them.[57]

Many reject the concept of a literal "fire and brimstone." Religions
such as Buddhism or Hinduism do not teach it. Groups such as
Jehovah's Witnesses and Christian Science reinterpret verse 10 to
avoid a literal interpretation. Generally, preachers who oppose
preaching what the Bible plainly states about an eternal Hell must
also find this chapter troubling.

Wilmington notes about the fiery torment to come, "Here is the
last hellfire-and-brimstone message that will ever be preached to
the unsaved, and it is delivered not by a Johnathan Edwards or a
Billy Sunday, but by and angel!"[58]

"Fire and brimstone" rained down upon Sodom and Gomorrah,
destroying both cities (Gen. 19:24). We should interpret the fire
of verse 10 as literal, not symbolic. Brimstone is the same burning
sulfur used in gunpowder and match sticks. The New Testament
repeatedly warns of a literal Hell. Chapters 19-20 provide more
details about the fiery torment to come.

> **Revelation 14:11** And the smoke of their tor-
> ment ascendeth up for ever and ever: and they
> have no rest day nor night, who worship the beast
> and his image, and whosoever receiveth the mark
> of his name.

Two phrases clearly state the concept:

- "**torment** ascendeth up **for ever and ever**"

- "no rest **day nor night**."

The fiery torment will be day and night for eternity. A false teaching
called the doctrine of annihilation teaches that this will not be

eternal torment but final fiery destruction. Verse 11 clearly states that the torment will have no end.

> **Revelation 14:12** Here is the patience of the saints: here are they that keep the commandments of God, and the faith of Jesus.

The judgment of those who persecute the saints during the tribulation will come. God encourages faithful obedience to his Word.

> **Revelation 14:13** And I heard a voice from heaven saying unto me, Write, Blessed are the dead which die in the Lord from henceforth: Yea, saith the Spirit, that they may rest from their labours; and their works do follow them.

John heard a voice he identified from heaven, "Yea, saith the Spirit." The Holy Spirit asks him to write this message of encouragement to those martyred for their faith.

God promises them "rest from their labours." God also promised **reward**, "their works do follow them." What a contrast to the future for those who have rejected Jesus Christ. There will be no rest from their suffering for all eternity (Rev. 14:11).

> **Revelation 14:14** And I looked, and behold a white cloud, and upon the cloud one sat like unto the Son of man, having on his head a golden crown, and in his hand a sharp sickle.

In John's day, the "sharp sickle" was a long, curved, razor-sharp iron blade used for reaping a harvest. Jesus used a similar illustration in one of his parables (see Matt. 13:39-42).

> **Revelation 14:15** And another angel came out of the temple, crying with a loud voice to him that sat on the cloud, Thrust in thy sickle, and reap:

for the time is come for thee to reap; for the harvest of the earth is ripe.

A prophecy from Joel is fulfilled by verse 15, "Put ye in the sickle,
for the harvest is ripe: come, get you down; for the press is full, the
vats overflow; for their wickedness is great. [14] Multitudes, multitudes in the valley of decision: for the day of the LORD is near in
the valley of decision" (Joel 3:13-14). Throughout Revelation, Old
Testament prophecies find their fulfillment.

> **Revelation 14:16** And he that sat on the cloud
> thrust in his sickle on the earth; and the earth
> was reaped.

The Earth is reaped in this harvest of judgment. Verses 17-20
describe a second harvest.

> **Revelation 14:17** And another angel came out
> of the temple which is in heaven, he also having
> a sharp sickle.

This fifth angel from the temple in Heaven brings "a sharp sickle."

> **Revelation 14:18** And another angel came out
> from the altar, which had power over fire; and
> cried with a loud cry to him that had the sharp
> sickle, saying, Thrust in thy sharp sickle, and
> gather the clusters of the vine of the earth; for
> her grapes are fully ripe.

This sixth angel "has power over fire," which may refer to the angel
in chapter 8 who took fire from the altar and cast it to the Earth
(Rev. 8:5). The imprecatory prayers of the martyrs were also offered
on this altar. Verse 18 records the answer to their prayers for justice.

When the "grapes are fully ripe" they are ready for harvesting.
Ryrie notes,

The picture here is that all false human religions are fully ripe and ready for harvest. Thus the harvest is ready because humankind in its own efforts, apart from the life of God, has fully developed an apostate religious system.[59]

> **Revelation 14:19-20** And the angel thrust in his sickle into the earth, and gathered the vine of the earth, and cast it into the great winepress of the wrath of God. [20] And the winepress was trodden without the city, and blood came out of the winepress, even unto the horse bridles, by the space of a thousand and six hundred furlongs.

John saw blood flow from the winepress "unto the horse bridles" or shoulder high. He mentions an area the size of 1,600 furlongs or about 200 miles, covering the entire region of Palestine. McArthur explains:

> A wine press consisted of two stone basins connected by a trough. Grapes would be trampled in the upper basin, and the juice would collect in the lower one. The splattering of the juice as the grapes are stomped vividly pictures the splattered blood of those who will be destroyed (cf. Isa. 63:3; Lam. 1:15; Joel 3:13).[60]

Lessons from Chapter 14:

- **Throughout the darkest spiritual time in history, the godly attributes and characteristics of the 144,000 should challenge every believer to ask God to make us more like Jesus.**

- **The unsaved may bow and take the mark of the beast to avoid the wrath of the Antichrist, but they will be unable to avoid God's wrath.**

- **The veil between this world and the eternal will grow thin as these end-times judgments lead our world toward the final judgment.**

## CHAPTER 14 OUTLINE

I. SONG OF THE REDEEMED 1-5

II. SAYINGS OF FINAL JUDGMENT 6-13

A. The Final Gospel

B. The Fall of Babylon

C. The Fiery Judgment

III. SICKLE OF LAST HARVEST 14-20

# CHAPTER 15

# THE SIGN OF THE LAST PLAGUES

## SIGN OF THE LAST PLAGUES

> **Revelation 15:1** And I saw another sign in heaven, great and marvellous, seven angels having the seven last plagues; for in them is filled up the wrath of God.

CHAPTER 11 RECORDED THE SOUNDING OF the seventh trumpet (Rev. 11:15). John has not recorded any events connected with that judgment. In chapter 15, John records the seven last plagues before the second coming of Jesus Christ.

The word "last" translates from *eschatos*, the original word behind our English word "eschatology" – the doctrine of last things.

The angels carry bowls "filled up" with God's undiluted wrath mentioned in chapter 14.

> **Revelation 15:2** And I saw as it were a sea of glass mingled with fire: and them that had gotten the victory over the beast, and over his image, and over his mark, and over the number of his name, stand on the sea of glass, having the harps of God.

Revelation 4:6 first mentioned the "sea of glass." These are the calm waters of life that will soon flow in the new kingdom. Chapter 22 records that it will become the River of Life. "And he showed me a pure river of water of life, clear as crystal, proceeding out of the throne of God and of the Lamb" (Rev. 22:1).

John described the sea "mingled with fire." The location is at the foot of God's throne, so the fire reflects the brilliant glory of God's presence.

John describes "them that had gotten the victory over the beast." These believers are faithful to the Lord, refusing to bow to the Antichrist. They never took the mark of the beast, or the number of his name – 666. The Antichrist thought he had defeated and destroyed them. Nevertheless, in God's eyes, they "had gotten the victory."

Their song is a song of victory, not defeat. As Stedman explained, "He imprisons, tortures, and murders the followers of Christ under the illusion that he is demonstrating his absolute power and ridding himself of his enemies. In reality, all he is doing is running a shuttle service to heaven!"[61]

> **Revelation 15:3** And they sing the song of Moses the servant of God, and the song of the Lamb, saying, Great and marvellous are thy works, Lord God Almighty; just and true are thy ways, thou King of saints.

The "song of Moses" was a song of deliverance and victory after crossing the Red Sea (Ex. 15, Deut. 32). These tribulation saints crossed over their own Red Sea into the promised land of Heaven victorious.

The "song of the Lamb" is a song of redemption (Rev. 5:9). Moses' song and the song of the Lamb are the **first and last songs** recorded in all of God's Word!

> **Revelation 15:4** Who shall not fear thee, O Lord, and glorify thy name? for thou only art holy: for all nations shall come and worship before thee; for thy judgments are made manifest.

Notice the contents of their praise:

- God's omnipotence

- God's holiness

- God's justice

- God's ways

Some question the fairness or justification of God's wrath upon our world. Each attribute of the Lord indicates why He alone is worthy to judge our world. After all their earthly afflictions, these tribulation believers still offer only praise to the Lord!

Psalm 86 prophesied: "All nations whom thou hast made shall come and worship before thee, O Lord; and shall glorify thy name. [10] For thou art great, and doest wondrous things: thou art God alone" (Ps. 86:9-10).

## GOLDEN VIALS OF WRATH

> **Revelation 15:5** And after that I looked, and, behold, the temple of the tabernacle of the testimony in heaven was opened:

The "tabernacle of the testimony" is the Old Testament title for the Tabernacle built in Moses' day containing the ark of the covenant (Ex. 38:21). Inside the golden ark was "the testimony," including the ten commandments written on two tablets of stone (Ex. 38:21). God commanded Moses to model the earthly Tabernacle after the design of the original one in Heaven. On Earth, the priests placed the ark in the Holy of Holies beyond the veil. "The temple" refers to God's heavenly Temple and his throne room.

> **Revelation 15:6** And the seven angels came out of the temple, having the seven plagues, clothed in pure and white linen, and having their breasts girded with golden girdles.

These angels come from God's heavenly Temple. In chapter 8, the seven angels blew the seven trumpets of judgment (Rev. 8:2).

> **Revelation 15:7** And one of the four beasts gave unto the seven angels seven golden vials full of the wrath of God, who liveth for ever and ever.

Zephaniah prophesied, "For my determination is to gather the nations, that I may assemble the kingdoms, **to pour upon them mine indignation**, even all my fierce anger: for all the earth shall be devoured with the fire of my jealousy" (Zeph. 3:8). The angels carry the vials or bowls of wrath in fulfillment of this prophecy.

> **Revelation 15:8** And the temple was filled with smoke from the glory of God, and from his power; and no man was able to enter into the temple, till the seven plagues of the seven angels were fulfilled.

When God's presence filled the tabernacle in the wilderness, "Moses was not able to enter into the tent of the congregation, because the cloud abode thereon, and the glory of the LORD filled the tabernacle" (Ex. 40:35). John is shown a similar scene during the tribulation. "No man was able to enter into the temple" until the final judgments were complete. There will no longer be any appeal or invitation to God's mercy seat during this final phase. God is dealing with sinful man in **his undiluted wrath**.

Lesson from Chapter 15:

- **Moses' song and the song of the Lamb are the first and last songs recorded in all of God's Word!**

- **Some may question the fairness or justification of the outpouring of God's wrath on our world. Each attribute of God indicates that he alone is worthy to judge our world.**

## OUTLINE OF CHAPTER 15

I. SIGN IN HEAVEN 1

II. SONG ON THE SEA OF GLASS 2-4

III. GOLDEN VIALS OF WRATH 5-8

## CHAPTER 16

# THE SEVEN VIALS OF WRATH

CHAPTER 16 REVEALS ALL SEVEN FINAL judgments and leads right up to the second coming of Jesus Christ. John describes the voice of the Lord from his heavenly Temple.

> **Revelation 16:1** And I heard a great voice out of the temple saying to the seven angels, Go your ways, and pour out the vials of the wrath of God upon the earth.

The trumpet judgments in chapter 8 have parallels in the vial judgments. The earlier judgments partially destroyed the land and water. The judgments of chapter 16 result in total and comprehensive destruction.

**WRATH OF DISEASE**

> **Revelation 16:2** And the first went, and poured out his vial upon the earth; and there fell a noisome and grievous sore upon the men which had the mark of the beast, and upon them which worshipped his image.

The first vial revealed "noisome and grievous" sores breaking out. One of Egypt's ten plagues was "the boil was upon the magicians, and upon all the Egyptians" (Exod. 9:11). The sores in this judgment will be burning, oozing, painful boils. Like the boils in Moses' day, this divine judgment **will not impact God's people.** The sores only affect those "which had the mark of the beast."

The first vial judgment is **boils.**

## WRATH ON THE DEPTHS

> **Revelation 16:3** And the second angel poured out his vial upon the sea; and it became as the blood of a dead man: and every living soul died in the sea.

This second vial causes the water in every sea to change. John warned, "it became as the blood of a dead man," killing all the living things in the seas. Revelation 8 prophesied the death of one-third of the sea creatures (Rev. 8:8-9). This judgment causes **all** surviving sea creatures to die. Dead fish will float to the surface and rot. Imagine the Gulf of Mexico, the eastern seaboard and the coastline of California covered with putrefying sea water and the corpses of dead fish. Disease and stench will contaminate the seas, the oceans, and the coastlines of much of the world. Chapter 21 describes the future earth without the seas (Rev. 21:1).

The second vial judgment is the **seas turned to blood.**

## WRATH ON DRINK

> **Revelation 16:4** And the third angel poured out his vial upon the rivers and fountains of waters; and they became blood.

The third vial judgment causes all the freshwater to become bloody, poisoned, and undrinkable. The judgment in chapter 8 caused the pollution of **one-third** of the freshwater and many died (Rev. 8:10-11). The freshwater from Niagara Falls to the Mississippi, from the Amazon River to the Nile will flow blood red. Imagine fresh-water lakes and springs all changed to diseased pools of blood.

A person in ideal conditions with excellent health can live without water for about a week. Conditions after so many stages of judgment and the scorching heat coming in verse 8, **reduce survivability to only days.**

Zechariah prophesied Jesus' dramatic return to the Mount of Olives, "and the mount of Olives shall cleave in the midst" (Zech. 14:4). Out of the mount will flow lifesaving, living water. "And it shall be in that day, that **living waters** shall go out from Jerusalem; half of them toward the former sea, and half of them toward the hinder sea: in summer and in winter shall it be" (Zech. 14:8). **The second coming of Jesus** provides the source of "living waters." By the end of God's judgments, the second coming of Jesus is **the only hope** for survival of all living things.

> **Revelation 16:5** And I heard the angel of the waters say, Thou art righteous, O Lord, which art, and wast, and shalt be, because thou hast judged thus.

John heard "the angel of the waters." Some angels have jurisdiction over various parts of our world. In chapter 7, angels held back the winds. The angel praises the Lord for his righteous judgment.

> **Revelation 16:6-7** For they have shed the blood of saints and prophets, and thou hast given them blood to drink; for they are worthy. [7] And I heard another out of the altar say, Even so, Lord God Almighty, true and righteous are thy judgments.

The loss of freshwater commences the final countdown for life on this Earth.

The Antichrist and his followers have such bloody hands. They are guilty of the murder of millions of God's children, the saints, and God's prophets. God's response is to send them "blood to drink." Akin comments about God's judgment:

> God is never arbitrary, capricious, or vengeful in His judgment. He is always fair, just, and true. His is the only bar of perfect justice. There is a logic and rightness in is judgment. We glorify Him in His righteous wrath.[62]

The third vial judgment is the destruction of **all freshwater**.

## WRATH OF DEGREES

> **Revelation 16:8** And the fourth angel poured out his vial upon the sun; and power was given unto him to scorch men with fire.

After the fouling of the world's water supply, the sun suffers judgment. Temperatures will rise, "to scorch men with fire." Isaiah indicates that God will turn up the heat seven-fold, "Moreover the light of the moon shall be as the light of the sun, and the light of **the sun shall be sevenfold**, as the light of seven days" (Isa. 30:26). Even lasting a few days, this heat could result in melting polar ice caps, destroying crops, second and third-degree burns, and many deaths.

> **Revelation 16:9** And men were scorched with great heat, and blasphemed the name of God, which hath power over these plagues: and they repented not to give him glory.

Malachi also prophesied about the heat of this coming judgment:

> For, behold, the day cometh, that **shall burn as an oven**; and all the proud, yea, and all that do wickedly, shall be stubble: and the day that cometh shall burn

them up, saith the LORD of hosts, that it shall leave them neither root nor branch (Mal. 4:1).

The fourth vial judgment is **the scorching heat**.

## WRATH OF DARKNESS

> **Revelation 16:10** And the fifth angel poured out his vial upon the seat of the beast; and his kingdom was full of darkness; and they gnawed their tongues for pain,

Three of the vial judgments impact the entire world. The fifth judgment only affects the Antichrist's kingdom. During the Exodus, God's people had light while the Egyptians were in darkness (Exod. 10:22-23). During this judgment, God's people have light in their wilderness protection, while the darkness the Antichrist's worshippers embrace tortures them.

The fifth vial judgment is **darkness** over the kingdom of the Antichrist.

> **Revelation 16:11** And blasphemed the God of heaven because of their pains and their sores, and repented not of their deeds.

Again, John describes sinful man's refusal to repent and the high cost of sin. Paul wrote about man's unrepentant spirit:

> Or despisest thou the riches of his goodness and forbearance and longsuffering; not knowing that the goodness of God leadeth thee to repentance? [5] But after thy hardness and impenitent heart treasurest up unto thyself wrath against the day of wrath and revelation of the righteous judgment of God; (Rom. 2:4-5).

In these final days of wrath, God's judgment remains righteous.

## WRATH ON DEFENSE

> **Revelation 16:12** And the sixth angel poured out his vial upon the great river Euphrates; and the water thereof was dried up, that the way of the kings of the east might be prepared.

"The great river Euphrates" forms the Promised Land's eastern boundary and the ancient boundary of the former Roman Empire. God could dry up the Red Sea (Ex. 14:21) or a strategic river. With the Euphrates River "dried up," the enemies from the east have a clear path toward the Antichrist and his forces.

Verse 14 prophecies that these "kings of the east" march their forces against Jerusalem in "the battle of that great day of God." Walvoord suggests who may lead this coming battle:

> The passage is best understood as referring to kings from, literally, the 'sun rising,' referring to Oriental rulers who will descend upon the Middle East in connection with the final world conflict described a few verses later. The massive specter of communist China alone, with its population of more than 1.3 billion people, makes such an invasion a reasonable prediction.[63]

> **Revelation 16:13** And I saw three unclean spirits like frogs come out of the mouth of the dragon, and out of the mouth of the beast, and out of the mouth of the false prophet.

John saw "unclean spirits" that were "like frogs" leap from the mouth of the dragon, the Antichrist, and the false prophet. The unholy trinity sends these evil spirits to gather their troops.

> **Revelation 16:14** For they are the spirits of devils, working miracles, which go forth unto

the kings of the earth and of the whole world, to gather them to the battle of that great day of God Almighty.

"The whole world" indicates another world war is coming. The Antichrist, his massive eastern armies, and worldwide military forces all gather to fight against Jesus and his heavenly armies. MacArthur describes some of the details:

> The mission of the demons is to gather not just the eastern powers, but all the world's rulers and armies to join the forces from the east for the war of the great day of God the Almighty. In their pride, arrogance, and folly, the demonically deceived nations of the world will converge on Palestine to do battle with God Himself at Armageddon.[64]

> **Revelation 16:15** Behold, I come as a thief. Blessed is he that watcheth, and keepeth his garments, lest he walk naked, and they see his shame.

Amid such dreadful judgment on this sin-sick world, the promise of Jesus's imminent Second Coming offers hope! Peter prophesied Jesus' return, "But the day of the Lord will come **as a thief** in the night; in the which the heavens shall pass away with a great noise, and the elements shall melt with fervent heat, the earth also and the works that are therein shall be burned up" (2 Pet. 3:10).

> **Revelation 16:16** And he gathered them together into a place called in the Hebrew tongue Armageddon.

"Armageddon" refers to Mount Megiddo and the surrounding Jezreel Valley in northern Israel. Megiddo is near Mount Carmel, the location of Elijah's fiery prayer before the prophets of Baal (1 Ki. 18:38-40). The valley of Megiddo has not seen battle for many years but is currently a World Heritage Site, on many Middle East tours.

Wiersbe noted, "Napoleon called this same area, "The most natural battlefield of the whole earth."[65] This is the location of Gideon's defeat of the Midianites, Saul's death, and King Josiah's defeat by the Egyptians.

The sixth vial judgment **prepares** for the Battle of Armageddon.

## WRATH OF DESTRUCTION

> **Revelation 16:17** And the seventh angel poured out his vial into the air; and there came a great voice out of the temple of heaven, from the throne, saying, It is done.

Jesus cried out, "It is finished" from the cross at Calvary (Jo. 19:30). Here he proclaims, "It is done." God completes the last outpouring of wrath in this final judgment. We have arrived at the Day of the Lord (Joel 1:15). Nothing else needs to occur before God can send His only Son back to this world to bring an end to the Antichrist's rule.

> **Revelation 16:18** And there were voices, and thunders, and lightnings; and there was a great earthquake, such as was not since men were upon the earth, so mighty an earthquake, and so great.

Isaiah prophesied these same events:

> Behold, **the day of the LORD** cometh, cruel both with wrath and fierce anger, to lay the land desolate: and he shall destroy the sinners thereof out of it. [10] For the stars of heaven and the constellations thereof shall not give their light: the sun shall be darkened in his going forth, and the moon shall not cause her light to shine. [11] And I will punish the world for their evil, and the wicked for their iniquity; and I will cause the arrogancy of the

proud to cease, and will lay low the haughtiness of the terrible (Isa. 13:9-11).

> **Revelation 16:19** And the great city was divided into three parts, and the cities of the nations fell: and great Babylon came in remembrance before God, to give unto her the cup of the wine of the fierceness of his wrath.

"The great city" is likely Jerusalem. In chapter 11, John called Jerusalem "the great city" (Rev. 11:8) and described an **earthquake** that partially destroyed it (Rev. 11:13). Stedman noted:

> Jerusalem is split into three parts by the derangement of the earth... There is a parallel description of this event in Zechariah 14, where the prophet tells us that the Mount of Olives will be split in half, part moving to the north, part to the south, creating a great valley between.[66]

"Great Babylon" is the Antichrist's capital city (see Ch. 17-18). God will remember her wickedness and will suddenly destroy Babylon in his wrath (Rev. 18:8).

> **Revelation 16:20** And every island fled away, and the mountains were not found.

"Every island fled away" indicates beautiful islands like the Bahamas, Hawaii, or Puerto Rico will all be gone. "Mountains were not found" also prophecies that inspiring mountains like the Blue Ridge, the Rockies, and the Himalayas will all be gone.

> **Revelation 16:21** And there fell upon men a great hail out of heaven, every stone about the weight of a talent: and men blasphemed God because of the plague of the hail; for the plague thereof was exceeding great.

The judgment of hail is like the plague that fell on Egypt during the Exodus (Exod. 9:23-26). The "weight of a talent" is about 100 pounds. Imagine the devastation caused by hailstones that weigh as much as a semi-truck tire raining from the skies.

Chronologically, the next event is the Second Coming of Jesus Christ, recorded in chapter 19. Chapters 17-18 provides important details about the Antichrist and his kingdom's judgment.

Lesson from Chapter 16:

- **The loss of freshwater starts the final countdown for life on this Earth. Neither man nor animal will survive long without fresh water.**

## CHAPTER 16 OUTLINE

I. WRATH OF DISEASE 1-2

II. WRATH ON THE DEPTHS 3

III. WRATH ON DRINK 4

IV. WRATH OF DEGREES 8-9

V. WRATH OF DARKNESS 10-11

VI. WRATH ON DEFENSE 12

VII. WRATH OF DESTRUCTION 17-21

## CHAPTER 17

# BABYLON THE GREAT, PART 1

I N THIS CHAPTER, JOHN IS SHOWN A VISION about the rise and fall of the Antichrist's kingdom. Like chapter 12, much of the chapter is symbolic, and the main characters in the vision require introduction and explanation.

- The Woman – represents the pagan idolatry of the new Babylon (Rev. 17:18).

- The Beast – represents the Antichrist and his kingdom (Rev. 13:1-4).

  Seven heads symbolize seven kings and their kingdoms preceding the Antichrist's future kingdom (Rev. 17:9-11).

  Ten horns represent ten kings briefly united under the Antichrist's rule (Rev. 17:12).

- The City of Babylon – represents both the headquarters of the one-world church (during the first half of the tribulation, Rev. 17:18), and the capital of the Antichrist's kingdom (during the second half of the tribulation).

## A WILDERNESS REVELATION

> **Revelation 17:1** And there came one of the seven angels which had the seven vials, and talked with me, saying unto me, Come hither; I will shew unto thee the judgment of the great whore that sitteth upon many waters:

John calls her "the great whore." He will reinforce the importance of this title by repeating it five times (See Rev. 17:5, 15, 16, and 19:2). This immoral term infers that the idolatrous religion she represents prostitutes itself to the leaders of the world.

Verse 1 also records she "sitteth upon many waters." People worldwide, "many waters," fall under her influence. More about the meaning of the water is explained in verse 15.

> **Revelation 17:2** With whom the kings of the earth have committed fornication, and the inhabitants of the earth have been made drunk with the wine of her fornication.

The woman prostitutes herself with "the kings of the earth" or the rulers of the world. The citizens of those same kingdoms are also "made drunk" on the fornication and wickedness of their evil relationship with her. Revelation 9 explained unbelievers during the tribulation embrace the worship of **devils, idolatry**, sorcery, and the fornication that accompanies each (Rev. 9:20-21).

Jeremiah also prophesied about this new Babylon, "Babylon hath been a golden cup in the LORD'S hand, that made **all the earth drunken**: the nations have drunken of her wine; therefore the nations are mad" (Jer. 51:7).

> **Revelation 17:3** So he carried me away in the spirit into the wilderness: and I saw a woman sit upon a

scarlet coloured beast, full of names of blasphemy, having seven heads and ten horns.

Royalty wears scarlet colored clothing. A scarlet cloak covers the horse of a king or queen (see Rev. 18:7). Riding the "scarlet coloured beast" indicates the woman's royalty. Once she fulfills her purpose, the Antichrist will no longer see her as necessary.

Her beast has "seven heads and ten horns," matching the description of the Antichrist and the ten kings under him (Rev. 13:1).

> **Revelation 17:4** And the woman was arrayed in purple and scarlet colour, and decked with gold and precious stones and pearls, having a golden cup in her hand full of abominations and filthiness of her fornication:

The "purple and scarlet" dress bejeweled with "gold and precious stones" represents the dress of Rome's wealthy and powerful. Money and power flow freely through the idolatrous church of the early tribulation period.

Verse 6 teaches more about the horrific contents of the "golden cup in her hand." Before addressing that, John offers more identification of the woman.

> **Revelation 17:5** And upon her forehead was a name written, MYSTERY, BABYLON THE GREAT, THE MOTHER OF HARLOTS AND ABOMINATIONS OF THE EARTH.

Consider the three identifying names John saw "upon her forehead:"

- **"Mystery"**— A mystery is a previously unknown or hidden truth. The idolatrous religious system represented by the woman was a "mystery" in John's day. John was aware of Rome's idolatry and the myriad of false gods and temples in the Roman empire. However, worldwide worship during the Antichrist's days will be unique in church history. Ryrie notes, "Since the true church is also called a mystery (Eph. 5:32), this apostate church is a counterfeit."[67]

- **"Babylon the Great"** – The last verse of this chapter explains, "the woman which thou sawest is that great city" (Rev. 17:18). The mystery woman symbolizes a religious system and her geographical center, a new city called Babylon.

- **"Mother of Harlots"** – Verse 1 names her "The Great Whore." This title shows her to be the first or "mother" of them all. Religious history demonstrates that ancient Babylonians worshipped Ishtar, their goddess of love. She is also called the Queen of Heaven and Mother of the gods. This term indicates her evil religion is the root of a system of idolatry and demon worship.

In the service of their goddess Ishtar, the Babylonians had temple prostitutes. In chapter 17, this immoral woman represents pagan idolatry promoted in ancient Babylon, practiced throughout all the ages, leading into the depths of its paganism during the seven years of the tribulation period.

Ladd commented about the rise of her paganism:

> Babylon is the 'mother of harlots.' She was not satisfied herself alone to entice men away from God; she insisted that her daughters join her in her nefarious and blasphemous designs. Along with her blasphemous harlotry she gave birth to all sorts of abominations which fill the earth.[68]

> **Revelation 17:6** And I saw the woman drunken with the blood of the saints, and with the blood of the martyrs of Jesus: and when I saw her, I wondered with great admiration.

John now records the contents of the golden cup she holds (Rev. 17:4). The cup contains "the blood" of the saints and martyrs of Jesus. Chapter 18 explains, "And in her was found **the blood of prophets**, and of saints, and of all that were slain upon the earth" (Rev. 18:24). Her anti-God, demon-worshipping idolatry is held responsible for killing God's faithful servants throughout the ages.

This dreadful sight was shocking to John. In over ninety years of life in the Middle East, he had never seen anything like this. John described his wonder and shock, "with great admiration" (not necessarily a positive response). The angel asked him about his reaction.

> **Revelation 17:7** And the angel said unto me, Wherefore didst thou marvel? I will tell thee the mystery of the woman, and of the beast that carrieth her, which hath the seven heads and ten horns.

After the angel asked John about his total shock, he offered a beneficial explanation.

> **Revelation 17:8** The beast that thou sawest was, and is not; and shall ascend out of the bottomless pit, and go into perdition: and they that dwell on the earth shall wonder, whose names were not written in the book of life from the foundation of the world, when they behold the beast that was, and is not, and yet is.

The type of pagan kingdom ruled by the Antichrist has existed in the past and will rise again. The angel explained, it "was, and is not, and shall ascend."

Throughout the seven-year tribulation, Satan's evil plan imitates God and his divine plan. By demonic deception, the devil will convince the tribulation world that the Antichrist died and then rose from the dead, imitating Christ's resurrection. Satan has no power to give life as Jesus does (John 10:18). The Antichrist's "resurrection" will be mere deception.

Satan's goal is for the world to bow and worship his puppet king, and in so doing fulfill Satan's desire to be worshipped (Isa. 14:13).

Akin notes about this verse:

> Verse 8 is the beast's parody on the life, death, and resurrection of the Lamb (1:18; 2:8; see also 1:4,8; 4:8). We see this in 13:3,14 as well. And yet there is embedded here an important truth that Christians of every age must understand. Throughout history multiple antichrists (1 John 2:18) have risen from the abyss in the form of the beast for their reign of terror. They have a time, they die, and then amazingly they appear again only to be destroyed. The pattern repeats itself again and again and will continue until the antichrist, the beast, brings the cycle to an end.[69]

The beast in verse 8 comes from "the bottomless pit," the same home to the locusts and their king, Abaddon (Rev. 9). The power and authority of the beast (the Antichrist) come from Satan.

John explains that this beast representing the Antichrist will "go into perdition," referring to his fiery judgment (Rev. 20:10). Paul also referred to the Antichrist as "the son of perdition" (2 Thess. 2:3).

> **Revelation 17:9-10** And here is the mind which hath wisdom. The seven heads are seven mountains, on which the woman sitteth. [10] And there are seven kings: five are fallen, and one is, and the other is not yet come; and when he cometh, he must continue a short space.

Verses 9 and 10 explain the meaning of the seven kings and their kingdoms. Daniel's vision describes five kingdoms: Egypt, Assyria,

Babylon, Persia, and Greece (see Dan. 11). In John's day, Rome was the current ruling empire, or the "one is." The "other is not yet come," refers to a future king and kingdom to follow Rome. Many suggest that the Roman Empire is a foreshadow or type of this coming kingdom.

> **Revelation 17:11** And the beast that was, and is not, even he is the eighth, and is of the seven, and goeth into perdition.

In verse 11, the seven heads represent seven kings and kingdoms. However, the verse clarifies that the Antichrist is not one of the seven but "even he is the eighth." Satan uses kings and their oppressive kingdoms throughout history. He constantly works to thwart God's plans and prevent the world from true faith. Satan's final attempt is "the eighth" kingdom. It is composed of all the evil components of the previous seven and led by the Antichrist.

> **Revelation 17:12** And the ten horns which thou sawest are ten kings, which have received no kingdom as yet; but receive power as kings one hour with the beast.

Under the Antichrist, ten kings rule for "one hour," or for a very brief period. They play a support role, particularly in the second half of the tribulation.

> **Revelation 17:13** These have one mind, and shall give their power and strength unto the beast.

These vassal or puppet kings give their power and authority to the Antichrist.

> **Revelation 17:14** These shall make war with the Lamb, and the Lamb shall overcome them: for he is Lord of lords, and King of kings: and they that are with him are called, and chosen, and faithful.

The "war with the Lamb" refers to the Battle of Armageddon (Rev. 16:16). Chapter 19 provides the details. This war is not fought by Christ alone. Those whose blood filled the cup held by the woman (Rev. 17:4) return with the Lamb for this battle (Rev. 19:14). Jesus promised that believers would be with Him always (Matt. 28:20). All of Heaven's angels with the resurrected believers follow Jesus to this great battle against the Antichrist.

> **Revelation 17:15** And he saith unto me, The waters which thou sawest, where the whore sitteth, are peoples, and multitudes, and nations, and tongues.

Sadly, all "peoples, and multitudes, and nations" will come under the seductive influence of the "Mother of Harlots." Throughout the world's history, there has always been a temptation to idolatrous worship. MacArthur explains the future problem with idolatry, "The harlot's authority will be universal; the entire world will be committed to the false worship of the Babylonian system, rather than the true God."[70]

## THE DEVASTATION OF THE WHORE

> **Revelation 17:16** And the ten horns which thou sawest upon the beast, these shall hate the whore, and shall make her desolate and naked, and shall eat her flesh, and burn her with fire.

These ten kings are united in their support of the Antichrist. Eventually, they will turn against the harlot and her one-world religion. Once the Antichrist reaches a point where she is no longer needed, he allows her to be destroyed. McGee offers a reason for their betrayal and her destruction:

> For a time, the Beast (Antichrist) is willing to share his place of exaltation with the harlot, since she has also sought to advance his cause while dividing his glory.

This he hates, and the ten kings are one with him in this. The Antichrist not only breaks his covenant with Israel, but he also breaks his relationship with the apostate church... By eliminating the apostate church, the way is cleared for the worship of Antichrist, as advocated by the False Prophet.[71]

> **Revelation 17:17** For God hath put in their hearts to fulfil his will, and to agree, and give their kingdom unto the beast, until the words of God shall be fulfilled.

God allows the Antichrist to rule the world for seven years (Dan. 9:27), but he still reigns from his heavenly throne. The destruction of the idolatrous system represented by the woman is God's plan.

> **Revelation 17:18** And the woman which thou sawest is that great city, which reigneth over the kings of the earth.

The angel states that the wicked woman also represents a city called Babylon, "that was, and is not, and yet is." The new city of Babylon is no longer the center of religion, however it continues to be the power center of Satan's demonic forces (Rev. 18:2).

Consider the hundreds of pagan religions in every country, led by thousands of false prophets, promoting the worship of millions of false gods, sacrificing at hundreds of millions of altars in cities worldwide. There is one primary purpose: to oppose the worship of the true God in spirit and in truth and to promote the worship of Satan's false gods in spiritual fornication and deception.

Lesson from Chapter 17:

- **The Antichrist's kingdom will cover the entire world and will bring every aspect of life under his evil control: a** one-world government, one-world economy, and one-world religion.

## OUTLINE OF CHAPTER 17

I. A WILDERNESS REVELATION 1-6 (Whore of Babylon)

  A.  Her Wealth 4

  B.  Her Wickedness 5

  C.  Her Wine 6

II. A WISE EXPLANATION 7-18 (The Antichrist)

  A.  The Description of the Beast 7-11 (7 Heads)

  B.  The Depiction of the Horns 12-14 (10 Horns)

  C.  The Detail of the Waters 15

  D.  the Devastation of the Whore 16-18

## CHAPTER 18

# BABYLON THE GREAT, PART 2

N OTICE THE LAST VERSE OF CHAPTER 17, "And the woman which thou sawest is that great city, which reigneth over the kings of the earth" (Rev. 17:18). The woman called "Mystery, Babylon the Great" (17:5) and "the great city of Babylon" (18:10) are **two aspects of one entity**.

- **The woman** – represents the pagan religious system, destroyed halfway through the Antichrist's reign (Rev. 17:16).

- **The city of Babylon** – becomes the center of power, riches, and immorality during the second half of the tribulation. God's judgment destroys Babylon toward the end of the seven-year reign of the Antichrist. Note the following side by side comparison of the two chapters supporting this:

| THE WOMAN (Ch. 17) | THE CITY (Ch. 18) |
|---|---|
| 17:2 drunk with wine of her fornication | 18:3 drunk with the wine of her fornication |
| 17:4 purple, scarlet, gold, pearls | 18:16 purple, scarlet, gold, pearls |
| 17:5 Babylon the Great | 18:2 Babylon the great |
| 17:18 that great city | 18:16 that great city |
| 17:6 blood of saints, martyrs | 18:24 blood of prophets, saints |
| 17:16 make her desolate | 18:19 is she made desolate |
| 17:16 burn her with fire | 18:8 burned with fire |
| 17:18 Kings of earth | 18:3 Kings of earth |

The angel provides a glimpse of the fall of the capital city of the Antichrist's kingdom.

## DECLARATION OF THE FALL OF BABYLON

> **Revelation 18:1** And after these things I saw another angel come down from heaven, having great power; and the earth was lightened with his glory.

Revelation is an informative book recording more about **angels and demons** than the rest of Scripture combined. Many of God's heavenly servants are creatures of "great power" and glory!

> **Revelation 18:2** And he cried mightily with a strong voice, saying, Babylon the great is fallen, is fallen, and is become the habitation of devils, and the hold of every foul spirit, and a cage of every unclean and hateful bird.

The **double emphasis** "is fallen, is fallen" indicates the **totality** of the fall.

In chapter 9, the release of about 200 million demons is prophesied (Rev. 9:13-16). Satan and his forces are defeated, banned from Heaven, and cast down to the Earth (Rev. 12:9). Imagine a single city becoming "the habitation of devils." Satan, his demons, and "every foul spirit" gather in the evil City of Babylon! Demonic forces possess the capital of the Antichrist's kingdom.

The words "hold" and "cage" are from the same original word. These foul spirits and unclean birds are kept in the city like caged animals in a zoo. Unclean birds such as vultures and carrion feed on the carcasses of the dead. These foul spirits gather to feed on the evil and wickedness that occurs in this city.

Isaiah described the judgment on this future Babylon:

It shall never be inhabited, neither shall it be dwelt in from generation to generation: neither shall the Arabian pitch tent there; neither shall the shepherds make their fold there. [21] But wild beasts of the desert shall lie there; and their houses shall be full of doleful creatures; and owls shall dwell there, and satyrs shall dance there (Isa. 13:20-21).

> **Revelation 18:3** For all nations have drunk of the wine of the wrath of her fornication, and the kings of the earth have committed fornication with her, and the merchants of the earth are waxed rich through the abundance of her delicacies.

All the nations and their leaders participate in the fornication and atrocities offered by the Antichrist. If we wonder what motivates such a globalist move, verse 3 indicates they "are waxed rich" off the Antichrist and his wealth-hoarding kingdom.

The many stages of judgment are sure to make life on Earth difficult. The Antichrist's control over all that is bought and sold (Rev. 13:16-17) causes severe shortages. Despite the devastating impact on the average person's lifestyle, the Antichrist's capital city gorges itself on licentiousness, gluttony, and fornication.

## REALIZATION OF THE FALL OF BABYLON

> **Revelation 18:4** And I heard another voice from heaven, saying, Come out of her, my people, that ye be not partakers of her sins, and that ye receive not of her plagues.

Jeremiah also voiced God's warning to flee the wickedness of Babylon. "Flee out of the midst of Babylon, and deliver every man his soul: be not cut off in her iniquity; for this is the time of the LORD'S vengeance; he will render unto her a recompence" (Jer. 51:6).

The Lord calls believers to "come out of her," avoiding her temptations to gain wealth and power. MacArthur commented:

> The biblical truth that believers are not to be involved in the world system will take on new urgency as Babylon faces imminent destruction. The angel's message to the believers still in that city is the same one that angels brought to Lot (Gen. 19:12-13): Get out before you are caught up in God's judgment of that wicked place.[72]

In verse 5, John records God's perspective on what precipitates the final judgment on Great Babylon.

> **Revelation 18:5** For her sins have reached unto heaven, and God hath remembered her iniquities.

Jeremiah also prophesied the overabundance of sin, "We would have healed Babylon, but she is not healed: forsake her, and let us go every one into his own country: for her judgment reacheth unto heaven, and is lifted up even to the skies" (Jer. 51:9).

Genesis records God's rejection of those who built the Tower of Babel, "Let us build us a city and a tower, whose top may reach unto heaven" (Gen. 11:4). God stopped the attempt to establish the first one-world religion in world history (Gen. 11:6). As the hardened bricks of that doomed tower were piled high, so the sins of the Antichrist's kingdom will also reach "unto heaven."

> **Revelation 18:6** Reward her even as she rewarded you, and double unto her double according to her works: in the cup which she hath filled fill to her double.

The call to reward "double unto her double" is like an Old Testament law that required the repayment of double what was lost or stolen (see Ex. 22:4,7,9). New Babylon and its paganism under the Antichrist deserve a double dose of God's wrath for the wickedness brought upon this world. Although others who take the mark of the beast will suffer, the Antichrist's kingdom should reap what she has sown. "Be not deceived; God is not mocked: for whatsoever a man soweth, that shall he also reap" (Gal. 6:7).

> **Revelation 18:7** How much she hath glorified herself, and lived deliciously, so much torment and sorrow give her: for she saith in her heart, I sit a queen, and am no widow, and shall see no sorrow.

With power, wealth, and rampant wickedness, national leaders lose all sense of shame or fear of consequences (1 Tim. 4:1-2). Convinced they "shall see no sorrow," they have no fear of judgment from God for their wickedness. We already see many of the social elite in our culture who have embraced this attitude and lifestyle. They have no apparent fear of consequences or of standing before God's great white throne to give an account (Rev. 20:11).

> **Revelation 18:8** Therefore shall her plagues come in one day, death, and mourning, and famine; and she shall be utterly burned with fire: for strong is the Lord God who judgeth her.

After thousands of years of plotting, devising, and undermining God's work, Satan is finally allowed to establish an evil kingdom and rule over the Earth. The Antichrist forces the entire world to worship his image or receive the death penalty. Within seven years, the Lord allows Satan's king and kingdom to rise to its height, and "in one day," it is destroyed.

Wiersbe considers how easily a new Babylon could collapse due to how connected everything is today:

> Certainly, the city of Rome was the center for world trade and government in John's day, and it was known for its extravagance and luxury. Politically and economically, the people in the empire were dependent

on Rome. Today, with the complex connections that exist between governments and businesses, and with the interrelated computer systems, it would not take long for 'Babylon' to collapse and the world's economic system to be destroyed.[73]

> **Revelation 18:9** And the kings of the earth, who have committed fornication and lived deliciously with her, shall bewail her, and lament for her, when they shall see the smoke of her burning,

## THE KINGS OF EARTH

The "kings of the earth" are mentioned 8 times in Revelation:

- They hide in caves for fear of God's wrath (Rev. 6:15).

- They follow the Antichrist to battle due to the spirits that went forth from the unholy trinity (Rev. 16:14).

- They commit spiritual fornication with the Woman, Babylon the Great (Rev. 17:2, 18:3, 18:9).

- They gather for the Battle of Armageddon (Rev. 19:19).

- During eternity in the New Heaven and Earth, godly kings bring their glory and honor to Jesus at the new Jerusalem (Rev. 21:24).

A common mistake is to assume the kings in verse 9 are the same "ten kings" from chapter 17. These leaders mourn the loss of the lavish, immoral things they indulged before the city's destruction.

The kings mourn Babylon's fall because the power and wealth they enjoyed came from this evil world empire.

> **Revelation 18:10** Standing afar off for the fear of her torment, saying, Alas, alas, that great city

Babylon, that mighty city! for in one hour is thy
judgment come.

We avoid getting too close when something terrible happens and
do not want to be associated with it. Peter followed Jesus to the trial
but stayed "afar off" (Lu. 22:54). These kings will keep their distance,
thinking they might avoid her judgment. They will face Jesus Christ
at the Battle of Armageddon to fight against him (Rev. 19:19).

> **Revelation 18:11** And the merchants of the earth
> shall weep and mourn over her; for no man buyeth
> their merchandise any more:

Since the mark of the beast forcibly controls all buying and selling
worldwide (Rev. 13:17), the merchants of the Antichrist's kingdom
become the richest in the world's history! The fall of Babylon is the
most significant economic collapse in world history.

> **Revelation 18:12-13** The merchandise of gold,
> and silver, and precious stones, and of pearls, and
> fine linen, and purple, and silk, and scarlet, and
> all thyine wood, and all manner vessels of ivory,
> and all manner vessels of most precious wood, and
> of brass, and iron, and marble, [13] And cinnamon,
> and odours, and ointments, and frankincense, and
> wine, and oil, and fine flour, and wheat, and beasts,
> and sheep, and horses, and chariots, and slaves,
> and souls of men.

Notice the seven hottest items available in the "International Bazaar
of Babylon." These items are not necessities but luxuries unavail-
able to the public. These priceless items will only be available to
those in power:

- Fine Jewelry – "gold,... silver,... precious stones"

- Fine Clothing – "fine linen,... silk"

- Fine Furniture – "thyine wood (or *citrim*, a citrus wood)... ivory, precious wood"

- Rare Perfumes – "cinnamon... odours"

- Fine Foods – "wine,... fine flour,... beasts"

- Top Transportation – "horses... chariots"

- Top Slaves – "slaves and the souls of men" (Rev. 18:13)

Under the Antichrist, one of the evil luxuries is **slaves**. The Antichrist's capital mixes the finest of luxuries with the evil of slavery, all marketed to and consumed by the "kings of Earth."

> **Revelation 18:14** And the fruits that thy soul lusted after are departed from thee, and all things which were dainty and goodly are departed from thee, and thou shalt find them no more at all.

Men will be so disappointed that "all things which were dainty and goodly" are no longer available. Satan loves to hold out a "shiny apple" and suggest that we want and need it. Just like Eve, people cannot wait to take a big bite (Gen. 3:6).

> **Revelation 18:15-18** The merchants of these things, which were made rich by her, shall stand afar off for the fear of her torment, weeping and wailing, [16] And saying, Alas, alas, that great city, that was clothed in fine linen, and purple, and scarlet, and decked with gold, and precious stones, and pearls! [17] For in one hour so great riches is come to nought. And every shipmaster, and all the company in ships, and sailors, and as many as trade by sea, stood afar off, [18] And cried when they saw the smoke of her burning, saying, What city is like unto this great city!

The destruction of Great Babylon, like the fall of ancient Babylon, will be shockingly sudden. Ryrie comments on the greed of the wealthy class:

> There will be a stock market crash and bankruptcy on a worldwide scale; yet, in the face of it, the thoughts of unsaved people will turn only to how their own interests are affected. This is selfishness and greed in its most naked form.[74]

The merchants and shipmaster's reaction is "weeping and wailing" due to their losses and the destruction of their top sales location.

Walvoord also contrasts the wealth of Babylon with true wealth:

> In contrast to the transitory wealth and glory of this world, which are here consumed by a great judgment from God, the true riches of faith, devotion, and service for God are safely stored in heaven beyond the destructive hands of man and protected by the righteous power of God. The destruction of Babylon also ends the nefarious control of human souls mentioned last in the list of commodities in verse 13. No longer can ancient Babylon control the world religiously, politically, or economically.[75]

## CELEBRATION OF THE FALL OF BABYLON

> **Revelation 18:20** Rejoice over her, thou heaven, and ye holy apostles and prophets; for God hath avenged you on her.

While ungodly leaders mourn over the fall of Babylon the Great, Heaven's reaction is to "Rejoice over her." The Lord calls for rejoicing over her judgment in answer to the martyr's cry, "how long?" (Rev. 6:10).

Another "mighty angel" provides a visual demonstration of the coming judgment.

> **Revelation 18:21** And a mighty angel took up a stone like a great millstone, and cast it into the sea, saying, Thus with violence shall that great city Babylon be thrown down, and shall be found no more at all.

A "millstone" was used to grind grain. Millstones are about four feet in diameter, twelve inches thick, and some weigh over 200 pounds! Jeremiah recorded a similar prophecy about the fall of Babylon:

> And it shall be, when thou hast made an end of reading this book, that thou shalt bind a stone to it, and cast it into the midst of Euphrates: 64 And thou shalt say, Thus shall Babylon sink, and shall not rise from the evil that I will bring upon her: and they shall be weary. Thus far are the words of Jeremiah (Jer. 51:63-64).

> **Revelation 18:22** And the voice of harpers, and musicians, and of pipers, and trumpeters, shall be heard no more at all in thee; and no craftsman, of whatsoever craft he be, shall be found any more in thee; and the sound of a millstone shall be heard no more at all in thee;

God's judgment brings a deathly silence to the streets of the Antichrist's capital city, once the center of world commerce.

> **Revelation 18:23-24** And the light of a candle shall shine no more at all in thee; and the voice of the bridegroom and of the bride shall be heard no more at all in thee: for thy merchants were the great men of the earth; for by thy sorceries were all nations deceived. 24 And in her was found the

blood of prophets, and of saints, and of all that were slain upon the earth.

No one lights "a candle" or lives within the walls of Babylon the Great ever again. The 1,000-year kingdom of Jesus Christ starts within days of her fall. As Jeremiah prophesied, during Christ's reign, Babylon the Great remains uninhabited, a pile of smoking ash:

> And they shall not take of thee a stone for a corner, nor a stone for foundations; but thou shalt be desolate for ever, saith the LORD. [29] And the land shall tremble and sorrow: for every purpose of the LORD shall be performed against Babylon, to make the land of Babylon a desolation without an inhabitant (Jer. 51:26, 29).

Notice three reasons highlighted for Babylon's judgment:

- "Thy merchants were the great men of the earth." The leaders of this world all participate in and profit from the sins of this city.

- "By thy sorceries were all nations deceived." Babylon deceives the nations with paganism, sorcery, and occultism. Millions of demons inhabiting the city cause overwhelming temptation for every inhabitant (Rev. 18:2).

- "In her was found the blood of prophets." God holds Satan's paganistic system responsible for murdering the prophets, the saints, and the martyrs.

Lessons from Chapter 18:

- **After thousands of years of plotting, deceiving, and undermining God's work, Satan will have his king and evil kingdom rule the Earth. Within seven years, it reaches its height, and "in one day," the Lord will destroy it!**

- **Satan loves to hold out a "shiny apple" and suggest that we really do want and even need it. Just like Eve, people cannot wait to take a big bite!**

## OUTLINE OF CHAPTER 18

I. DECLARATION OF THE FALL OF BABYLON 1-3

II. REALIZATION OF THE FALL OF BABYLON

   A.  Realized by Believers 4-8

   B.  Realized by Kings 9-10

   C.  Realized by Merchants 11-19

III.CELEBRATION OF THE FALL OF BABYLON 20-24

## CHAPTER 19

# THE BATTLE OF ARMAGEDDON

THIS FANTASTIC CHAPTER PUTS THE TWO women of Revelation side by side:

- The Whore of Babylon (Rev. 19:2) – also called the unholy city of Babylon which is indwelt by demonic evil
- The Bride of Christ (Rev. 19:7-9) – also called the new Jerusalem, indwelt by all the redeemed (Rev. 21:9-10)

This chapter also puts the two feasts of Revelation side by side:

- The Marriage Feast of the Lamb and His Bride (Rev. 19:9)
- The disgusting Feast of the Fowl (Rev. 19:17-18)

Chapter 19 brings the reader to the most anticipated event of history: The return of the Lamb of God as the King of Kings!

**PRAISE FOR THE JUDGMENT OF CHRIST**

> **Revelation 19:1** And after these things I heard a great voice of much people in heaven, saying, Alleluia; Salvation, and glory, and honour, and power, unto the Lord our God:

Consider who is in this Heavenly crowd "great voice of much people:"

- Patriarchs like Abraham, Isaac, & Jacob

- Prophets like Samuel, Elijah, & Daniel

- Kings like David, Solomon, & Josiah

- The Gospel writers Matthew, Mark, Luke, and John, the beloved disciple who wrote Revelation!

**Alleluia** is a transliterated word from the original Greek *allelouia*. It means "Praise Jehovah!" The word only appears four times in the Bible, all in Revelation chapter 19 regarding Christ's second coming!

> **Revelation 19:2** For true and righteous are his judgments: for he hath judged the great whore, which did corrupt the earth with her fornication, and hath avenged the blood of his servants at her hand.

Verse 2 brings another charge against the Whore of Babylon (Rev. 17:5). The Lord holds her pagan, idolatrous system guilty of corrupting or defiling the entire world. Our world looks at paganism as just another belief system or a different religious option. The church in America hardly considers idolatry a relevant issue. However, God looks upon all forms of idolatry as Satan's religion, corrupting the world and defiling all who participate.

> **Revelation 19:3** And again they said, Alleluia. And her smoke rose up for ever and ever.

God allows the "smoke" from Babylon's destruction to rise "for ever and ever" as a testimony and reminder of her judgment. Isaiah also described it:

> And the streams thereof shall be turned into pitch, and the dust thereof into brimstone, and the land thereof

shall become burning pitch. [10] It shall not be quenched night nor day; the smoke thereof shall go up for ever: from generation to generation it shall lie waste; none shall pass through it for ever and ever (Isa. 34:9-10).

> **Revelation 19:4** And the four and twenty elders and the four beasts fell down and worshipped God that sat on the throne, saying, Amen; Alleluia.

Chapter 11 contains the previous mention of "the four and twenty elders," right after the seventh trumpet. Verse 4 is the last reference to these distinguished believers whom we look forward to meeting one day.

## PREPARATION OF THE BRIDE OF CHRIST

> **Revelation 19:5-6** And a voice came out of the throne, saying, Praise our God, all ye his servants, and ye that fear him, both small and great. [6] And I heard as it were the voice of a great multitude, and as the voice of many waters, and as the voice of mighty thunderings, saying, Alleluia: for the Lord God omnipotent reigneth.

In response to the call to praise the Lord "all ye his servants" (Rev. 19:5), praise begins in verses 6-8. The psalmist gave the same prophetic call to praise, "The LORD reigneth; let the earth rejoice;" (Ps. 97:1). The prophecies of Revelation are guaranteed fulfillment because "the Lord God omnipotent reigneth." Even during the Antichrist's reign for a few years on Earth, the all-powerful God still reigns.

> **Revelation 19:7** Let us be glad and rejoice, and give honour to him: for the marriage of the Lamb is come, and his wife hath made herself ready.

The "marriage of the Lamb" precedes the "marriage supper" coming up in verse 9. To understand this prophetic event, consider some historical Jewish wedding background.

- At the betrothal, the man gives a ring to the young lady, vows to marry her (the marriage vows as we would know them) and signs a marriage covenant (*ketubah*) before witnesses.

- After the betrothal, the groom returns to his father's house and spends up to a year adding on a room (*chadar*) for his bride. The groom's father supervises this meticulous work of preparation.

- The father determines when to send his son to get his bride. The bride works during this time, preparing herself and her bridesmaids for the groom's arrival. They keep lamps lit in their windows until the day the groom comes for the bride (Matt. 25:3-4).

- On the day of the wedding, the friends of the bridegroom travel to the bride's home to announce that the bridegroom is on his way (Matt. 25:6). The bridegroom's arrival is preceded with music, shouting, and celebration.

- The bridesmaids accompany the bride to the groom's home. Outside the new home, the bride and groom stand beneath a silken canopy (*chuppah*), for the wedding ceremony.

- After blessings are recited the entire party moves to the wedding feast. The feast usually last about seven days.[76]

Verse 7 indicates that it was time for "marriage of the Lamb." The groom prepared the wedding home. Jesus told his disciples, "I go to prepare a place for you..." (John 14:2). The groom's arrival will soon be announced. The bride and her bridesmaids prepare for that day. Soon, the groom is informed that the bride "has made herself ready."

## Who is the Bride of the Lamb?

- **The Church** is commonly considered the Bride of Christ (Eph. 5:23-25). Due to Paul's reference in Ephesians, many suggest that the "bride of the Lamb" refers to the Church. However, the Church is not the focus of chapters 4 through 22. The Church is part of the Bride, but not the whole of her.

- **Israel** is also called the wife of the Lord. "For thy Maker is thine husband; the LORD of hosts is his name; and thy Redeemer the Holy One of Israel;" (Isa. 54:5). However, interpreting the bride to represent Israel excludes those who are not Jewish. If the bride is only the church, then Israel is excluded. The author suggests another option.

- Chapter 21 states that the bride of the Lamb is the city of new Jerusalem and **all its inhabitants**:

  And I John saw the holy city, new Jerusalem, coming down from God out of heaven, prepared as a bride adorned for her husband (21:2) Come hither, I will **show thee the bride**, the Lamb's wife... and showed me that great city, **the holy Jerusalem**, descending out of heaven from God (Rev. 21:9-10).

New Babylon is the unholy capital city of the Antichrist, filled with demonic inhabitants. The new Jerusalem is the holy capital city of God filled with heavenly inhabitants. Chapter 21 reveals that this city's citizens are "they which are written in the Lamb's book of life" (Rev. 21:27). **The redeemed of all the ages** will come into this holy city, which is called "the bride, the Lamb's wife" (Rev. 21:9-10).

> **Revelation 19:8** And to her was granted that she should be arrayed in fine linen, clean and white: for the fine linen is the righteousness of saints.

In contrast to the scarlet and purple of the whore of Babylon, the bride of Christ will wear a pure, "clean and white" wedding gown.

"The righteousness of saints" composes the material of the bride's gown. The psalmist also described, "As for me, I will behold thy face in righteousness: I shall be satisfied, when I awake, with thy likeness" (Ps. 17:5). The prophet Isaiah declared,

> I will greatly rejoice in the LORD, my soul shall be joyful in my God; for he hath clothed me with the garments of salvation, he hath covered me with the robe of righteousness, as a bridegroom decketh himself with ornaments, and as a bride adorneth herself with her jewels (Isa. 61:10).

> **Revelation 19:9** And he saith unto me, Write, Blessed are they which are called unto the marriage supper of the Lamb. And he saith unto me, These are the true sayings of God.

The length of a Jewish wedding supper depends on the wealth of the host. Some last one evening, while others continue for a week. Those "called unto the marriage supper of the Lamb" may enjoy a wedding feast lasting 1,000 years! As believers in Jesus Christ, celebrate your reservation for this marriage supper and not for the awful feast of flesh coming up in verses 17-18.

> **Revelation 19:10** And I fell at his feet to worship him. And he said unto me, See thou do it not: I am thy fellowservant, and of thy brethren that have the testimony of Jesus: worship God: for the testimony of Jesus is the spirit of prophecy.

We can imagine the joy John felt hearing such good news after so many dark visions of God's wrath. The angel reminds John that worship should only be given to the one true God, "worship God."

Some practice **angel worship**, which the Lord forbides (Matt. 4:9-10; Rom. 1:25; Col. 2:18; Rev. 22:8-9).

Osborne notes:

> As John is about to worship the angel, he is told severely that only God is worthy of worship. Angelolatry (the worship of angels) is a form of idolatry. This has relevance for the fad today to place angels on too high a pedestal. We must remember that they are not higher beings than us; they are in reality our 'fellow servants,' so long as we continue to 'serve' God by maintaining our 'testimony about Jesus.'[77]

## PROCLAMATION OF THE COMING OF CHRIST

> **Revelation 19:11** And I saw heaven opened, and behold a white horse; and he that sat upon him was called Faithful and True, and in righteousness he doth judge and make war.

The description in verse 11 is vastly different from Paul's description of the Rapture (1 Thess. 4:15-17). The Second Coming follows the last judgment, perhaps even the same day (see Matt. 24:27-30; Mark 13:24-26).

In chapter 1, John wrote about the Second Coming of Jesus and those who see him. "Behold, he cometh with clouds; and every eye shall see him, and they also which pierced him: and all kindreds of the earth shall wail because of him. Even so, Amen" (Rev. 1:7). Jesus' Second Coming will be so different from the sudden gathering and removal of believers at the Rapture (I Thess. 4:14-18). Everyone will see him, but not all will welcome his appearance (Rev. 6:15-17).

Jesus also prophesied his return and the mourning of the unsaved. "And then shall appear the sign of the Son of man in heaven: and then shall all the tribes of the earth mourn, and they shall see the Son of man coming in the clouds of heaven with power and great glory" (Matt. 24:30).

> **Revelation 19:12** His eyes were as a flame of fire, and on his head were many crowns; and he had a name written, that no man knew, but he himself.

Verse 12 begins John's description of our Lord's appearance for the final battle. Each aspect of his appearance is filled with great meaning.

The eyes of the Lord glow with flames of the coming judgment on the Antichrist and his kingdom. Isaiah wrote, "For, behold, the LORD will come with fire, and with his chariots like a whirlwind, to render his anger with fury, and his rebuke with flames of fire" (Isa. 66:15).

The *diadema* or diadem is not a single crown but is composed of "many crowns," representing the King of kings. Freeman explained:

> Monarchs who claimed authority over more than one country wore more than one crown. The kings of Egypt were crowned with the *psheni*, or united crowns of Upper and Lower Egypt. When Ptolemy Philometer entered Antioch as a conqueror, he wore a triple crown, two for Egypt, and the third for Asia. John saw him who was 'King of kings and Lord of lords,' and 'on his head were many crowns.' Thus, in a beautiful figure, the universal dominion of our blessed Lord is set forth.[78]

John announces that Jesus has "a name written, that no man knew." Jesus is God in the flesh. There is much about Him beyond comprehension. Look for three more names which will all be of great significance.

> **Revelation 19:13** And he was clothed with a vesture dipped in blood: and his name is called The Word of God.

Since verse 13 is before the upcoming battle with the Antichrist, we might wonder why he wears a "vesture dipped in blood." There are three possible interpretations:

- Blood of the Lamb shed for our salvation (Rev. 5:9)

- Blood of the martyrs shed by the Lord's enemies (Rev. 6:10)

- Blood of the Lord's enemies (Rev. 14:20)

Isaiah's prophecy offers several parallels which aid in understanding the vesture.

> "Wherefore art thou red in thine apparel, and thy garments like him that treadeth in the winefat?" ³ "... for I will tread them in mine anger, and trample them in my fury; and their blood shall be sprinkled upon my garments, and I will stain all my raiment" (Isa. 63:2-3).

The prophecy from Isaiah clarifies that the blood is that of the Lord's enemies.

At his Second Coming, Jesus will be called "The word of God," a name from before creation began (Jo. 1:1, 14). Verses 15 and 21 describe a sword from the Lord's mouth. Jesus is the Word of God, even if God's wrath is outpoured in judgment.

> **Revelation 19:14** And the armies which were in heaven followed him upon white horses, clothed in fine linen, white and clean.

Jesus promised that believers will be with Him always (John 14:3). Believers from all ages follow Jesus and join this mighty army dressed in robes of the righteousness of Christ, "white and clean."

**Revelation 19:15** And out of his mouth goeth
a sharp sword, that with it he should smite the
nations: and he shall rule them with a rod of iron:
and he treadeth the winepress of the fierceness
and wrath of Almighty God.

In chapter 1, the "sharp sword" from the Lord's mouth is called
a "sharp twoedged sword" (Rev. 1:16). The nations gathered at
this battle are "smitten" with this sword. "The remnant" of unbelievers bearing the mark of the beast are slain (Rev. 19:21). After
the Rapture and twenty-six stages of the God's wrath on our world
over half will be gone.

Jesus will lead the nations as a shepherd with a "rod of iron." The
Psalmist wrote prophetically about the Lord's enemies, "Thou shalt
break them with a rod of iron; thou shalt dash them in pieces like
a potter's vessel." [12] "Kiss the Son, let he be angry, and ye perish
from the way, when his wrath is kindled but a little" (Psa. 2:9,12).

**Revelation 19:16** And he hath on his vesture and
on his thigh a name written, KING OF KINGS,
AND LORD OF LORDS.

Jesus is coming as "King of Kings, and Lord of Lords" to defeat
Satan and his Antichrist.

**Revelation 19:17-18** And I saw an angel standing
in the sun; and he cried with a loud voice, saying
to all the fowls that fly in the midst of heaven,
Come and gather yourselves together unto the
supper of the great God; [18] That ye may eat the
flesh of kings, and the flesh of captains, and the
flesh of mighty men, and the flesh of horses, and
of them that sit on them, and the flesh of all men,
both free and bond, both small and great.

The vultures and other carrion come to this second detestable feast, anticipating the upcoming battle. Akin explains that God will be indiscriminate in his judgment:

> Kings, captains, and mighty men will be judged. Free and slave will be judged. Just as our God is indiscriminate in His offer of salvation (Acts 10:34), He is also without discrimination in His judgment. A day of universal, righteous reckoning is coming. Everyone will be held accountable for their rejection of the Lamb.[79]
>
> > **Revelation 19:19** And I saw the beast, and the kings of the earth, and their armies, gathered together to make war against him that sat on the horse, and against his army.

The Antichrist and his armies gather for the battle against the Lord (Rev. 16:16). There are two parts to the battle:

- the capture of the Antichrist (Rev. 19:20)
- the destruction of his evil hosts (Rev. 19:21)

Details about the battle are better understood with information from several Old Testament prophecies:

## THE BATTLE OF ARMAGEDDON–OLD TESTAMENT PROPHECIES

- God causes the Antichrist's forces to gather in the Valley of Jehoshaphat beneath the Mount of Megiddo. Joel prophesied, "Assemble yourselves, and come, all ye heathen,..." [12] "Let the heathen be wakened, and come up to the valley of Jehoshaphat: for there will I sit to judge all the heathen round about" (Joel 3:11-12).

- Jesus Christ returns in all His power and glory to the Mount of Olives. Zechariah provides the details:

Then shall the LORD go forth,...[4] And his feet shall stand in that day upon the mount of Olives, which is before Jerusalem on the east, and the mount of Olives shall cleave in the midst thereof toward the east and toward the west, and there shall be a very great valley; and half of the mountain shall remove toward the north, and half of it toward the south (Zech. 14:3-4).

- The Lord orders His forces from Jerusalem to the battle. Joel provides the details. "The LORD also shall roar out of Zion, and utter his voice from Jerusalem; and the heavens and the earth shall shake:" (Joel 3:16).

- The Lord comes to the battle in the fury of his fiery judgment to destroy his enemies. Isaiah described the battle.

For the indignation of the LORD is upon all nations...
[3] Their slain also shall be cast out, and their stink shall come up out of their carcases, and the mountains shall be melted with their blood (Isa. 34:2-3).

> **Revelation 19:20-21** And the beast was taken, and with him the false prophet that wrought miracles before him, with which he deceived them that had received the mark of the beast, and them that worshipped his image. These both were cast alive into a lake of fire burning with brimstone. [21] And the remnant were slain with the sword of him that sat upon the horse, which sword proceeded out of his mouth: and all the fowls were filled with their flesh.

After seven years of murder, death, and deceit the Antichrist brought upon our world, verse 20 describes his fall with five words: **"and the beast was taken."** The world empire of the Antichrist quickly comes to an end.

The Antichrist and the False Prophet are cast alive into "a lake of fire burning with brimstone." Verse 20 does not describe their annihilation. They "were cast **alive**." There are five references to the Lake of Fire, all found in the book of Revelation (Rev. 19:20, 20:10, 20:14, 20:15, 21:8). The Antichrist and False Prophet are the first two to be cast alive into this place of eternal judgment. Chapter 20 explains more about the Lake of Fire.

Lesson from Chapter 19:

- **The length of a Jewish wedding supper depended on the wealth of the host. Those "called unto the marriage supper of the Lamb" may enjoy a wedding feast lasting 1,000 years!**

- **After seven years of murder, death, and deceit the Antichrist brought upon our world, verse 20 describes his fall with five words: "and the beast was taken."**

## OUTLINE CHAPTER 19

I. PRAISE FOR THE JUDGMENT OF CHRIST 1-4

II. PREPARATION OF THE BRIDE OF CHRIST 5-10

III. PROCLAMATION OF THE COMING OF CHRIST 11-21

A. Christ's Glorious Appearance

B. Call to Gather Armies

C. Conquest at Armageddon

## CHAPTER 20

# FINAL THINGS

BABYLON, THE CAPITAL CITY OF SATAN'S empire is destroyed. The Antichrist and the False Prophet have been thrown alive into the Lake of Fire. In the next vision, John sees Jesus Christ standing in Jerusalem, crowned as King of Kings and Lord of Lords. What is his first command? What will the first order of business be on the first day of his thousand-year reign on Earth?

**FETTERS FOR SATAN**

> **Revelation 20:1-2** And I saw an angel come down from heaven, having the key of the bottomless pit and a great chain in his hand. ²And he laid hold on the dragon, that old serpent, which is the Devil, and Satan, and bound him a thousand years,

Jesus' first command in his new kingdom is to bind the Devil with "a great chain" and lock him up!

Other demons are also chained awaiting their judgment. Jude wrote that God has already chained some fallen angels due to their disobedience. "And the angels which kept not their first estate, but left their own habitation, he hath reserved in everlasting chains under darkness unto the **judgment** of the great day" (Jude 6).

Chapter 12 recorded the same names for Satan, "And the great dragon was cast out, that old serpent, called the Devil, and Satan" (Rev. 12:9).

> **Revelation 20:3** And cast him into the bottomless pit, and shut him up, and set a seal upon him, that he should deceive the nations no more, till the thousand years should be fulfilled: and after that he must be loosed a little season.

The Romans tried to seal Christ's tomb (Matt. 27:66). They attempted to keep Jesus' dead body in the tomb Joseph provided (Matt. 27:59-60). Although Satan, Governor Pilate, and the soldiers guarding his tomb tried to keep Jesus dead and buried, they failed. Jesus arose on that third day (1 Cor. 15:4). In contrast, Satan is defeated and locked away for 1,000 years. Walvoord comments on the length of time. "This passage introduces, for the first time in Scripture, the exact length of Christ's earthly kingdom. Six times in this passage, the fact is stated that the period is a thousand years or a millennium."[80]

Davids addressed the issue of Satan's imprisonment:

> God appears to have a use for Satan, but not in the immediate future. He is used for the final probation of human beings after God has demonstrated his just rule. Thus Satan is not kept out of hell for his own sake, but is reserved for God's own good purposes...[81]

During the next millennium, Satan will "deceive the nations no more." Imagine a world no longer under the influence of the same Devil who tempted Eve (Gen. 3:1).

## FIRST RESURRECTION

> **Revelation 20:4** And I saw thrones, and they sat
> upon them, and judgment was given unto them:
> and I saw the souls of them that were beheaded
> for the witness of Jesus, and for the word of God,
> and which had not worshipped the beast, neither
> his image, neither had received his mark upon
> their foreheads, or in their hands; and they lived
> and reigned with Christ a thousand years.

Verse 4 records "thrones" and those who ruled from them. Chapter
5 looked forward to this event. "And hast made us unto our God
kings and priests: and we shall reign on the earth" (Rev. 5:10).
Jesus prophesied that the twelve apostles are among these rulers,
reigning over the twelve tribes of Israel. "When the Son of man
shall sit in the throne of his glory, ye also shall sit upon twelve
thrones, judging the twelve tribes of Israel" (Matt. 19:28). Many
others will also receive crowns of glory and share in Christ's reign
(2 Tim. 2:12, Rev. 20:6, 22:5).

The martyrs of the tribulation have a unique role in Christ's
Kingdom. "And they overcame him by the blood of the Lamb...
and they loved not their lives unto the death" (Rev. 12:11).

Notice the emphatic restatement of "a thousand years" (Rev. 20:2, 3,
4, 5, 6). Some claim that the Millennial Kingdom of Christ on earth
is symbolic and taught nowhere in Scripture. Yet, the 1,000 years
is written a total of six times in this context. The repetition indicates the significance and literalness of this prophecy regarding the
period of Christ's reign!

> **Revelation 20:5** But the rest of the dead lived not
> again until the thousand years were finished. This
> is the first resurrection.

Who are "the rest of the dead?" They will not reign with Christ, nor will they serve as priests of God or Christ.

Revelation divides God's creation into two groups: those in the first resurrection and those in the second death. In John's Gospel, Jesus explained the same concept of two resurrections. "And shall come forth; they that have done good, unto **the resurrection of life**; and they that have done evil, unto **the resurrection of damnation**" (John 5:29).

Two groups are in mind here:

- Believers who are part of the first resurrection unto life.
- Unbelievers who are part of the second death (v 6).

> **Revelation 20:6** Blessed and holy is he that hath part in the first resurrection: on such the second death hath no power, but they shall be priests of God and of Christ, and shall reign with him a thousand years.

The first death is the **physical death.** The second death refers to eternal death: **eternal existence without God.** Verse 14 explains, "And death and hell were cast into the lake of fire. This is the second death." Chapter 21 also connects the Lake of Fire to the second death. "Shall have their part in the lake which burneth with fire and brimstone: which is the second death" (Rev. 21:8).

The first resurrection results in a judgment determining believer's rewards. Some will become priests of the Lord, while others will rule over part of Christ's kingdom. Jesus taught the disciples how to pray, "Thy Kingdom come thy will be done in earth as it is in heaven" (Matt. 6:10), and this prayer request becomes a reality! Revelation does not give us many details about the Millennium Kingdom, but the Old Testament prophets fill in those gaps:

# OLD TESTAMENT PROPHECY REGARDING THE MILLENNIAL KINGDOM

- Living Water flows from Jerusalem to the Dead Sea & the Mediterranean Sea (Zech. 14:8).

- The deserts bloom and become like the Garden of Eden (Ezek. 36:33-38).

- Pre-flood conditions return, and life spans are extremely long (Isa. 65:20-25).

- People and animals enjoy an Eden-like co-existence, the lamb rests together with the lion (Isa. 11:4-9).

- There may be one world language again (Zeph. 3:9).

- Jesus Christ rules from Jerusalem, the Millennial Kingdom's world capital (Jer. 3:17).

- The shekinah glory of the Lord fills the Temple (Ezek. 43:1-7).

- Righteousness and peace reign (Psa. 72:6-8).

- There is no more war, and all nations come to Jerusalem to worship Jesus (Isa. 2:2-4).

- Jerusalem becomes the city of truth (Zech. 8:1-8).

- Nations refusing to come and worship the Lord will not receive rain (Zech. 14:17-19).

One could easily spend another entire book considering the wonders of life on Earth during the Millennial Kingdom.

## FINAL BATTLE

> **Revelation 20:7-8** And when the thousand years are expired, Satan shall be loosed out of his prison, ⁸ And shall go out to deceive the nations which are in the four quarters of the earth, Gog

and Magog, to gather them together to battle: the number of whom is as the sand of the sea.

In the Old Testament, "Gog and Magog" were kingdoms north of Israel, such as Russia. But notice the symbolic use in verse 8, "the nations which are in the four quarters of the earth," indicating the entire world!

At the end of 1,000 years with King Jesus, one might wonder how Satan deceives the nations again. Most assume all unbelievers die at the Battle of Armageddon (Rev. 19:21). The author suggests that many are born during the thousand-years Christ reigns on Earth. The children grow up and enjoy life on Earth without war in an Eden-like existence seeing King Jesus in the flesh. Yet generation after generation must personally accept salvation by faith in Jesus. Even in a near perfect environment without Satan's deceptive influence, everyone will not choose the free gift of salvation (Rom. 6:23).

Ironside notes this pattern over the ages of man:

Tested *in the garden of delight* man broke through the only prohibition laid upon him. Tested under *conscience*, corruption and violence filled the earth, and the scene had to be cleared by the deluge. Tested under the restraining influence of divinely appointed *government*, man went into idolatry, thus turning his back upon his Creator. Tested under *law*, he cast off all restraint and crucified the Lord of Glory. Tested under *grace* in this current dispensation of the Holy Spirit, he has shown himself utterly unable to appreciate such mercy and has rejected the Gospel and gone ever deeper into sin. Test under the *personal reign* of the Lord Jesus Christ for a thousand years, some people will be ready to listen to the voice of the tempter when, at the close, he ascends from the pit of the Abyss bent upon one last defiant effort to thwart the purpose of God. It is a melancholy history indeed and emphasizes the truth that the heart of man is incurably evil.[82]

> **Revelation 20:9** And they went up on the breadth of the earth, and compassed the camp of the saints about, and the beloved city: and fire came down from God out of heaven, and devoured them.

The Lord releases Satan one final time, and he deceives many to follow him against Jesus in Jerusalem. Satan stirs armies from around the world to follow him to battle one last time. What an incredible prophecy of man's fallen condition. Even after one thousand years without Satan's deception, unsaved man rejects Christ as Lord and chooses to follow Satan.

The final battle is fought and won in an instant. Fiery judgment falls from Heaven, and the final war is over! This is the final record of the last chapter of this world's history as we know it.

> **Revelation 20:10** And the devil that deceived them was cast into the lake of fire and brimstone, where the beast and the false prophet are, and shall be tormented day and night for ever and ever.

The Antichrist and his sidekick have been in the place of eternal torment during the previous thousand years (Rev. 19:20). Satan now joins them in eternal fire. However, he is not the only one deserving judgment. Look closely at the following verses – some of the **most sobering in the entire Bible**!

## FINAL JUDGMENT

Notice the description of a Judge in this courtroom scene.

**Revelation 20:11** And I saw a great white throne, and him that sat on it, from whose face the earth and the heaven fled away; and there was found no place for them.

It is fearful to stand guilty before a judge in any local court. It is terrifying to stand before a judge in a federal court. We cannot begin to imagine the feeling of standing before the great white throne, face to face with our Creator, the Lord God.

John describes "the earth and the heaven fled away." Chapters 21 and 22 teach about a new Heaven and Earth. The old war-torn Earth and the current Heaven cease to exist. Jesus taught that Heaven and Earth would pass away. "Heaven and earth shall pass away, but my words shall not pass away" (Matt. 24:35).

Peter also wrote about when God makes a new Heaven and Earth:

> Looking for and hasting unto the coming of the day of God, wherein the heavens being on fire shall be dissolved, and the elements shall melt with fervent heat? [13] Nevertheless we, according to his promise, look for new heavens and a new earth, wherein dwelleth righteousness (2 Pet. 3:12-13).

Notice the evidence presented in the heavenly court.

**Revelation 20:12** And I saw the dead, small and great, stand before God; and the books were opened: and another book was opened, which is the book of life: and the dead were judged out of those things which were written in the books, according to their works.

Those following Satan to the final battle are "devoured" by fire from Heaven. That is not the final judgment for them. Although there is no second chance (such as some teach about Purgatory), they stand before God for final judgment and sentencing.

An examination of the Lord's sacred records begins this trial. Heaven's hall of records contains details of all sinful thoughts, words, and deeds. Verse 12 warns about judgment "according to their works." Even works done in secret are on record, as Paul wrote, "In the day when God shall judge the secrets of men by Jesus Christ..." (Rom. 2:16).

The book of works provides evidence of sinfulness. There are no errors in the record and nothing hidden or unknown to God. The Lord's judgment of works has nothing to do with our salvation. Believer's work establishes their rewards (2 Cor. 5:10). The Lord uses the works of unbelievers to choose various degrees of punishment. Jesus gives an example in Matthew 11, "It shall be **more tolerable** for Tyre and Sidon at the day of judgment, than for you" (Matt. 11:22).

Akin comments on the trial and punishment:

> Here is a theological principle we must not miss: At the great white throne, every single person will be judged fairly and equally. But the people there will not all receive the same penalty and punishment. Everyone will be 'thrown into the lake of fire' (20:15; 21:8), but there will be varying degrees of punishment and suffering.[83]

Missing in Heaven's sacred records are **the sinful deeds of born-again believers.** By their simple faith in Jesus and his shed blood on Calvary:

- Jesus bore all our sins to his cross (1 Pet. 2:24) and has forgiven us (Col. 1:14)

- He removed our sins from us (Psa. 103:12)

- He cast our sin "into the depths of the sea" (Mic. 7:19)

- He remembers our sin no more (Heb. 8:12)

John saw "another book" called "the book of life" (cf. Rev. 13:8). If one's name appears in Who's Who or on the cover of Time magazine has no impact on the judgment. It only matters that your name appears in the **Book of Life** of the Lamb of God. Eternal life is God's gift for simple, saving faith in Jesus Christ (John 3:18). Verse 15 clarifies, "whosoever was not found written in the book of life was cast into the lake of fire."

> **Revelation 20:13** And the sea gave up the dead which were in it; and death and hell delivered up the dead which were in them: and they were judged every man according to their works.

Jesus holds the keys to death and Hell (Rev. 1:18). Everyone stands before Jesus as Judge. The rich man waiting in Hell, tormented by the flames, and begging the saved beggar for a drop of water, will finally be freed only to stand before Jesus at the great white throne (Luke 16:23-24).

No unbeliever escapes this judgment. All those who hate Christ curse His holy name and oppose God and His people give account to Jesus. Paul wrote about Jesus as Judge, "Before God, and the Lord Jesus Christ, who shall judge the quick and the dead at his appearing and his kingdom;" (2 Tim. 4:1).

Jesus also judges believers (Rom. 14:10-12; 2 Cor. 5:10). The Lord is not judging them to determine punishment since their sins are forgiven and removed from Heaven's records. Like the finish line judge at the Olympics, believer's works determine eternal rewards (1 Cor. 3:13-14). The Lord rewards believers with treasurers they laid up in Heaven (Matt. 6:19-20).

In verse 13, John revealed the Judge, the Lord Jesus Christ, and John explained the evidence against sinful man. Lastly, notice the sentencing phase.

> **Revelation 20:14** And death and hell were cast into the lake of fire. This is the second death.

Chapter 21 describes eternity in which there will be no more "death" (Rev. 21:4). Verse 14 indicates Hell no longer exists. In the end, there is only the Lake of Fire. Verse 14 provides the last of 54 references to Hell in the Bible. McGee explained:

> 'Hades,' the prison of lost souls, is likewise cast into the lake of fire. The lost are no longer in hades but in the lake of fire. This is where Satan, the wild Beast, the False Prophet, and their minions were consigned. If man will not accept the life of God, he must accept the only other alternation: eternal association with Satan.[84]

Verse 6 mentions "the second death." Verse 14 puts the two types of death in context. All of us experience physical death (Heb. 9:27). The Lake of Fire awaits those whose names are not in the Lamb's Book of Life. That destiny is their "second death."

> **Revelation 20:15** And whosoever was not found written in the book of life was cast into the lake of fire.

What a contrast between "Whosoever will may come" (Rev. 22:17) and whosoever in verse 15! Even those who may stand before Jesus and claim they went to church, served God, and had even done miracles in His name are sent to a devil's eternity because they rejected Jesus as their personal Savior. Jesus warned, "Many will say to me in that day, Lord, Lord, have we not prophesied in thy name? and in thy name have cast out devils? and in thy name done many wonderful works? [23] And then will I profess unto them, I never knew you: depart from me, ye that work iniquity" (Matt. 7:22).

In the new Jerusalem, there is a river of life flowing from the throne of God. In contrast, John saw "the lake of fire." Jesus explained that he prepared this lake for his archenemies. "Depart from me, ye cursed, into everlasting fire, prepared for the devil and his angels:" (Matt. 25:41). Satan and all his fallen angels belong in this eternal fire (Rev. 20:10). Some may trivialize an eternity in this place and boast about seeing others there. But the reality is an endless nightmare: living in darkness without God, suffering unending fiery torment, and sharing this place with the Devil, the demons, and the Antichrist for all eternity.

Jesus prophesied this day of fiery judgment. "And shall cast them into a furnace of fire: there shall be wailing and gnashing of teeth." (Matt. 13:42).

Lessons from Chapter 20:

- **Even in a near perfect environment without Satan's deceptive influence, everyone will not choose the free gift of salvation (Rom. 6:23).**

- **Some might be surprised to discover that in Heaven's record, the Lord will not find the sinful deeds of born-again believers.**

- **If one's name appeared in Who's Who or on the cover of Time magazine has no importance at this judgment. It only matters that your name appears in the Book of Life of the Lamb of God by simple, saving faith in Jesus Christ (John 3:18).**

# OUTLINE OF CHAPTER 20

I. FETTERS FOR SATAN 1-3

II. FIRST RESURRECTION 4-6

III. FINAL BATTLE 7-10

    A. The Deception 7-8

    B. The Doom 9-10

IV. FINAL JUDGMENT

    A. The Judge 11

    B. The Evidence 12-13

    C. The Sentence 14-15

## CHAPTER 21

# THE NEW JERUSALEM

**THE GRACE OF ETERNITY**

> **Revelation 21:1** And I saw a new heaven and a
> new earth: for the first heaven and the first earth
> were passed away; and there was no more sea.

CHAPTER 21 RECORDS THE NEW TESTAMENT version of Genesis 1:1, "In the beginning God created the heaven and the earth." The Lord starts Creation again, but this time without Genesis 3: no more snake in the Garden!

John saw that the new Earth has "no more sea." Water currently covers two-thirds of the Earth. Without the oceans, there are no more boundaries between continents and much more inhabitable space. The crystal river of life from God's throne replaces the ocean waters.

> **Revelation 21:2** And I John saw the holy city, new
> Jerusalem, coming down from God out of heaven,
> prepared as a bride adorned for her husband.

Since John described the new Jerusalem as "coming down from God out of heaven," he reminds us that Jesus said he was leaving his disciples to go "prepare a place for you" (Jo. 14:2).

> **Revelation 21:3** And I heard a great voice out of
> heaven saying, Behold, the tabernacle of God is
> with men, and he will dwell with them, and they
> shall be his people, and God himself shall be with
> them, and be their God.

One of Jesus' wonderful names is "Emmanuel" meaning "God is with men." Matthew recorded Joseph's dream about the angel's announcement of Jesus' birth, "They shall call his name Emmanuel, which being interpreted is, God with us" (Matt. 1:23). In verse 3, at the beginning of eternity, that promise becomes a reality.

> **Revelation 21:4** And God shall wipe away all
> tears from their eyes; and there shall be no more
> death, neither sorrow, nor crying, neither shall
> there be any more pain: for the former things
> are passed away.

In chapter 7, one of the twenty-four elders told John, "God shall wipe away all tears from their eyes" (Rev. 7:17). The Psalmist looked forward to this glorious day, "For thou hast delivered my soul from death, mine eyes from tears, and my feet from falling" (Ps. 116:8). Isaiah spoke of our victory with the Lord, "He will swallow up death in victory; and the Lord God will wipe away tears from off all faces" (Isa. 25:8). All that so many suffered, the tears grievously shed are over and replaced with the Lord's comforting presence.

Another way God ends his children's tears is that the *protos* or "former things" are passed away. No more sin or suffering, Satan is gone, and our loved ones will no longer die. All things will finally "become new" (2 Cor. 5:17).

> **Revelation 21:5** And he that sat upon the throne
> said, Behold, I make all things new. And he
> said unto me, Write: for these words are true
> and faithful.

The Creator makes a new Heaven and new Earth, and believers enjoy resurrected bodies just like Jesus (1 Jo. 3:2). The only thing that never changes is God (Heb. 13:8).

> **Revelation 21:6** And he said unto me, It is done. I am Alpha and Omega, the beginning and the end. I will give unto him that is athirst of the fountain of the water of life freely.

Jesus said on the cross, "It is finished," the price of sin is paid in full (John 19:30). Here at the beginning of eternity, the Lord proclaims, "It is done:"

- The sin of Adam in the garden is over.

- Satan, his destructive deceit, and his evil temptations of humanity is ended.

- Man's rejection of God as Creator, his walk in darkness, and his worship of gods of his own making are over.

- Jesus closed the seven-sealed book of God's final wrath on this World.

- The fallen Earth that groaned for deliverance (Rom. 8:21-22) is "passed away."

Jesus, who made all things (Jo. 1:3), creates a "new heaven and a new earth." Eternity and all its promise and glory begin!

John bore record of Jesus' invitation, "If any man thirst, let him come unto me, and drink. [38] He that believeth on me, as the scripture hath said, out of his belly shall flow rivers of living water" (John 7:37-38). Here in chapter 21, the promise of giving the "water of life" is reiterated.

> **Revelation 21:7** He that overcometh shall inherit all things; and I will be his God, and he shall be my son.

Heaven is not only for those who successfully live up to God's righteous standards. The Old Testament law proves that man is born with a sinful nature making a sinless life impossible (Rom. 3:20). Man cannot save himself by any amount of good living (Rom. 3:12). Heaven is for all who overcome by faith in Jesus Christ and his sacrifice on the cross (1 Pet. 1:18-19). In John's first letter, he wrote, "For whatsoever is born of God overcometh the world: and this is the victory that overcometh the world, **even our faith**" (1 Jo. 5:4).

As God's children, believers are joint-heirs with Jesus (Rom. 8:17). In eternity we will "inherit all things." Paul wrote, "The Spirit itself beareth witness with our spirit, that we are the children of God: [17] And if children, then heirs; heirs of God, and joint-heirs with Christ" (Rom. 8:16-17).

John introduced his Gospel with the promise of eternity together as God's children. "But as many as received him, to them gave he power to become the sons of God, even to them that believe on his name:" (Jo. 1:12). As adopted sons and daughters of God, every believer should joyfully anticipate the privilege of being "an heir of God through Christ" (Gal. 4:5-7).

> **Revelation 21:8** But the fearful, and unbelieving, and the abominable, and murderers, and whoremongers, and sorcerers, and idolaters, and all liars, shall have their part in the lake which burneth with fire and brimstone: which is the second death.

This verse does **not** say that those who rejected Jesus Christ have a second chance or that they have time in purgatory and then hope to go on to Heaven. The concept of a half-way stop before Heaven or Hell is nowhere in the Word of God! Jesus said that the rich man died, "And in hell he lift up his eyes being in torments" (Luke 16:22-23). The scripture records no second chance to leave such a place after death.

The first on the list is "the fearful," those who fear men but not God (Matt. 10:28). The second is "the unbelieving" (Jo. 3:18). One could live a good, moral, religious life and miss Heaven due to their unbelief in Jesus (Matt. 7:21-22). Jesus warned Nicodemus, "he that believeth not is condemned already, because he hath not believed in the name of the only begotten Son of God" (Jo. 3:18).

The final one on the "second death" list raises concern for many: "and all liars." We all agree that the average Christian deserves the same eternity as the unsaved (Rom. 3:23). Every believer is thankful that Christ's sacrifice on the cross satisfied God's judgment in full for all our sin (1 Pet. 2:24).

John described the grace of eternity as seen in God's presence and God's people. The remainder of this chapter describes the glory of eternity.

## THE GLORY OF ETERNITY

> **Revelation 21:9** And there came unto me one of the seven angels which had the seven vials full of the seven last plagues, and talked with me, saying, Come hither, I will shew thee the bride, the Lamb's wife.

John records two terms, "the bride" and "the Lamb's wife." The use of **both** terms indicates that the angel is speaking very specifically. Chapter 20 mentions the wedding of the Bride of the Lamb. Here comes the Bride!

> **Revelation 21:10** And he carried me away in the spirit to a great and high mountain, and shewed me that great city, the holy Jerusalem, descending out of heaven from God,

This verse states that **the Lamb's Bride is the new Jerusalem** with all its blessed inhabitants. Verses 12 and 14 clarify that the citizens include believers from Israel and the Church.

> **Revelation 21:11-12** Having the glory of God: and her light was like unto a stone most precious, even like a jasper stone, clear as crystal; ¹² And had a wall great and high, and had twelve gates, and at the gates twelve angels, and names written thereon, which are the names of the twelve tribes of the children of Israel:

John saw angels standing guard at each of the twelve gates to the city. Saint Peter is not the doorman at Heaven's gate to let us in. Daniel recorded that Michael is the angel God assigned over Israel (Dan. 12:1). He will be among the angels welcoming those who enter these gates.

Believing Jews from each tribe enter into the city through the gate of their tribe. Abraham longed to find this city "which hath foundations, whose builder and maker is God" (Heb. 11:10).

> **Revelation 21:13-14** On the east three gates; on the north three gates; on the south three gates; and on the west three gates. ¹⁴ And the wall of the city had twelve foundations, and in them the names of the twelve apostles of the Lamb.

The apostles laid the Church's foundation (Eph. 3:20) and will serve as kings over the twelve tribes (Matt. 19:28). Their names appear on the "twelve foundations" of this glorious city. Believers who form the Body of Christ, the Church, dwell in the new Jerusalem. Saved Jews and Gentiles, both as children of God, together become the beautiful Bride of the Lamb in the new Jerusalem. Together they enjoy eternity in the home Christ himself prepared!

> **Revelation 21:15-16** And he that talked with me had a golden reed to measure the city, and the gates thereof, and the wall thereof. [16] And the city lieth foursquare, and the length is as large as the breadth: and he measured the city with the reed, twelve thousand furlongs. The length and the breadth and the height of it are equal.

Some suggest "the city lieth foursquare" indicates a perfect cube. The Holy of Holies is a perfect cube: 20 cubits (about 30 feet), by 20 cubits by 20 cubits (1 Kings 6:10, 20). The new Jerusalem may be a perfect expansion of the Holy of Holies, God's heavenly throne room, brought down to the new Earth for redeemed man to dwell with him.

One side of the city is 12,000 furlongs or *stadia,* the original word for stadium or racecourse. This measure amounts to 1500 miles on each side. LaHaye described it,

> Thus the city itself would stretch from about the eastern seaboard of the United States to the Mississippi River on one side and from the Canadian border to the Gulf of Mexico on the other.[85]

The largest city in the United States by area is Juneau, Alaska, covering an impressive 3,081 square miles. The new Jerusalem covers 2,250,000 square miles!

The top floor of the city will be 1500 miles high. Commercial planes only fly 10 miles from the ground, and the record space shuttle orbit is less than 400 miles high. For perspective, the space shuttle orbits about 25% of the way to the top of this new city.

Imagine such an immense structure, made not of steel but out of **solid gold**. Estimates are that a city this size could offer over **20 Billion residents** one cubic mile each for their mansions!

> **Revelation 21:17** And he measured the wall thereof, an hundred and forty and four cubits, according to the measure of a man, that is, of the angel.

The wall John saw around the city is 144 cubits. The length of the king's forearm determines the size of the cubit. The wall is approximately 200 feet high surrounding the entire city.

> **Revelation 21:18** And the building of the wall of it was of jasper: and the city was pure gold, like unto clear glass.

The wall around the city is made of jasper, a brilliant stone like our diamond.

> **Revelation 21:19-20** And the foundations of the wall of the city were garnished with all manner of precious stones. The first foundation was jasper; the second, sapphire; the third, a chalcedony; the fourth, an emerald; [20]The fifth, sardonyx; the sixth, sardius; the seventh, chrysolite; the eighth, beryl; the ninth, a topaz; the tenth, a chrysoprasus; the eleventh, a jacinth; the twelfth, an amethyst.

Jewelers use many of these precious stones in valuable rings or jewelry. The High Priest's breastplate is decorated with these precious stones (Ex. 28:15-20). Imagine the beauty that emanates as the light of God's glory pours through transparent walls and bejeweled foundations of this glorious city.

> **Revelation 21:21** And the twelve gates were twelve pearls; every several gate was of one pearl: and the street of the city was pure gold, as it were transparent glass.

We pave streets with asphalt or concrete. Jesus built the city streets and walls of the new Jerusalem of pure transparent gold. The beauty and glory of the city Jesus is preparing stretch our wildest imagination.

> **Revelation 21:22** And I saw no temple therein: for the Lord God Almighty and the Lamb are the temple of it.

The Old Testament law limits access to the Holy Temple. Only the priests are allowed into the Holy Place (Ex. 28:43), and only the High Priest is allowed beyond the veil once per year into the Holy of Holies (Ex. 26:33-34). In the new Jerusalem, every believer has open access to the very presence of the Lord!

> **Revelation 21:23** And the city had no need of the sun, neither of the moon, to shine in it: for the glory of God did lighten it, and the Lamb is the light thereof.

John reveals that there is longer a Sun in the new sky since God's glory provides all the light that this new Heaven and Earth need.

> **Revelation 21:24-25** And the nations of them which are saved shall walk in the light of it: and the kings of the earth do bring their glory and honour into it. <sup>25</sup> And the gates of it shall not be shut at all by day: for there shall be no night there.

John mentions "the nations" in this verse, indicating that new Jerusalem is the capital city. There are other cities on the new Earth, ruled by other kings. These kings come to new Jerusalem, bringing "their glory and honour" to Christ.

In John's day, the gates of every city are closed and locked each sundown. The Lord never closes the twelve gates of pearl, guarded by angels. There is no more night, no thieves, and no crime. Jesus, the light of the World, never leaves as God makes His forever home with every believer.

> **Revelation 21:26-27** And they shall bring the glory and honour of the nations into it. [27] And there shall in no wise enter into it any thing that defileth, neither whatsoever worketh abomination, or maketh a lie: but they which are written in the Lamb's book of life.

Osborne commented about the lack of a Temple:

> There is no temple because all that was signified in the earthly temple (the presence of God and the relationship between him and his people) are now finalized, so the temple is indeed God and the Lamb with his people (21:22). There is no need for external sources of light (21:23,25) because God's Shekinah glory and the presence of the Lamb illumine the city. Therefore, all the glory of the nations are surrendered to God.[86]

We learned in Chapter 20 what eternity has in store for those who reject Christ. The defiled and those who rejected truth have their part in the Lake of Fire. The citizens of the new Jerusalem, the city of gold, include all those who believed in Jesus Christ as their Savior.

Lesson from Chapter 21:

- **Heaven is not for only those who successfully live up to God's righteous standards. No one would make it! Heaven is for all those who overcome through faith in Jesus Christ.**

# OUTLINE OF CHAPTER 21

## I. THE GRACE OF ETERNITY 1-8

A. Grace in God's Presence 1-3

B. Grace on God's People 4-8

## II. THE GLORY OF ETERNITY 9-27

A. The Eternal Light of the City 9-21

    1. Its Majesty 9-14

    2. Its Measure 15-17

    3. Its Magnificence 18-21

B. The Eternal Life of the Citizens 22-27

## CHAPTER 22

# EVEN SO, COME

**Revelation 22:1-2** And he shewed me a pure river of water of life, clear as crystal, proceeding out of the throne of God and of the Lamb. ² In the midst of the street of it, and on either side of the river, was there the tree of life, which bare twelve manner of fruits, and yielded her fruit every month: and the leaves of the tree were for the healing of the nations.

JESUS OFFERS THE "PURE RIVER OF WATER OF life" to all who thirst (Rev. 21:6). In eternity, the river's source is God's throne, "out of the throne of God and of the Lamb."

McGee comments about the River of Life:

> There was a river in the first Eden which branched into four rivers. Although there was abundance of water, it is not called the water of life. Eden was a garden of trees among which was the Tree of Life. God kept the way open for man by the shedding of blood (see Gen. 3:24). In the new Jerusalem there is a river of the Water of Life, and the throne of God is its living fountain supplying an abundance of water.[87]

The "tree of life" first appears in Genesis 2. The Lord forbade Adam and Eve from ever touching the tree after their sin (Gen. 3). Citizens enjoy the twelve life-giving fruits from this tree growing next to the river of life.

John mentions that the leaves of the tree of life will be for "the healing of the nations." The word "healing" is from the word *therapeia* (the origin behind our word for therapy), indicating **health**. Since there is no more pain or death (Rev. 21:4), our resurrected bodies do not require any healing in the typical sense of the meaning, but the tree of life provides healthiness.

> **Revelation 22:3** And there shall be no more curse: but the throne of God and of the Lamb shall be in it; and his servants shall serve him:

The "curse" of sin began in Genesis 3 with Adam's disobedience (Gen. 3:17). That curse impacts the ground, causing the earth to produce thorns and weeds (Gen. 3:18). The curse of sin results in physical death (Gen. 3:19) and spiritual death without Jesus Christ (Rom. 6:23). The curse causes sinful man to be separated from holy God until Jesus came as the sacrificial Lamb of God to save us (1 Pet. 2:24). Through Jesus' sacrifice on Calvary, there is "no more curse."

Most wonder what life is like during eternity. Many Hollywood images intentionally mock and deride those who believe in life after death. Chapters 21 and 22 provide the Lord's best description of the grace, peace, and joy of sinless life with Jesus. Believers are all active, involved in praise, and enjoying all the privileges of serving the Lord for eternity.

> **Revelation 22:4** And they shall see his face; and his name shall be in their foreheads.

Moses asked Jehovah God to "see his face" (Ex. 33:20). After the resurrection, believers enjoy resurrected bodies like Jesus after he rose from the dead. The Lord designed our new bodies for our eternal existence (see 1 Cor. 15). We enjoy the privilege of seeing "his face," basking in God's glorious presence, bearing the same seal or stamp the 144,000 received for all eternity (Rev. 7:3, 9:4).

> **Revelation 22:5** And there shall be no night there; and they need no candle, neither light of the sun; for the Lord God giveth them light: and they shall reign for ever and ever.

There is "no night there." Physically, the presence of the Lord is the light. In the spiritual sense, the darkness of sin will not stain our eternity. The glory and holiness of God and the Lamb light our eternal life with him forever.

> **Revelation 22:6-7** And he said unto me, These sayings are faithful and true: and the Lord God of the holy prophets sent his angel to shew unto his servants the things which must shortly be done. [7] Behold, I come quickly: blessed is he that keepeth the sayings of the prophecy of this book.

Jesus said, "I come quickly." Notice other references in chapter 22:

- Verse 10, "the time is at hand"
- Verse 12, "behold, I come quickly"
- Verse 20, "Surely I come quickly"

The words "shortly" and "quickly" are from the same original Greek word. No time or date is given for the beginning of these things. "But of that day and hour knoweth no man, no, not the angels of heaven..." (Matt. 24:36). These verses do not suggest a time frame. When Jesus' Second Coming occurs, these events happen quickly or **suddenly**.

Would Jesus have us believe any other way? Peter wrote, "Knowing this first, that there shall come in the last days scoffers, walking after their own lusts, ⁴ And saying, Where is the promise of his coming?" (2 Pet. 3:3). His imminent return is the hope to which believers cling! His sudden coming in the clouds is the believer's motivation to continue in our faithfulness!

Verse 7 reminds us to consider what the Lord expects while we wait for His return. He promised a blessing, "blessed is he that keepeth the sayings." Notice the same emphasis again in verse 14, "Blessed are they that do his commandments." **Jesus expects us to keep His word**, to fulfill his commands while waiting expectantly for his return. Happiness in this life and blessings in eternity is found by those who show him their love, "If ye love me, keep my commandments" (John. 14:15).

> **Revelation 22:8-9** And I John saw these things, and heard them. And when I had heard and seen, I fell down to worship before the feet of the angel which shewed me these things. ⁹ Then saith he unto me, See thou do it not: for I am thy fellowservant, and of thy brethren the prophets, and of them which keep the sayings of this book: worship God.

John had a previous "worship error" in chapter 19, just before the Second Coming of Jesus (Rev. 19:10). Twice, in John's transparent writing, he admits to this mistake. During the temptation of Jesus in the wilderness, the Lord quotes from the Old Testament, "Thou shalt worship the Lord thy God, and him only shalt thou serve" (Luke 4:8).

MacArthur comments on worship in Revelation:

> Calling the bewildered apostle back to the one and only object of worship, the angel commanded John to worship God. A proper understanding of Revelation

should elicit worship; thus, **worship is a major theme in the Apocalypse** (cf. 4:8-11; 5:8-14; 7:9-12; 15:2-4; 19:1-6). As noted above, God alone is the only acceptable Person to worship. The Bible forbids the worship of anyone else, including angels, saints, the Virgin Mary, or any other created being (cf. Col. 2:18).[88]

> **Revelation 22:10** And he saith unto me, Seal not the sayings of the prophecy of this book: for the time is at hand. [11] He that is unjust, let him be unjust still: and he which is filthy, let him be filthy still: and he that is righteous, let him be righteous still: and he that is holy, let him be holy still.

Each of us is on a path toward one destiny or the other:

- Those who are unjust or filthy

- Those who are righteous or holy.

Some such as "he that is righteous...," are on a path leading to life with God (Matt. 7:14). Others described as "he which is filthy" are on the broad way toward eternal separation from God (Matt. 7:13).

> **Revelation 22:12-15** And, behold, I come quickly; and my reward is with me, to give every man according as his work shall be. [13] I am Alpha and Omega, the beginning and the end, the first and the last. [14] Blessed are they that do his commandments, that they may have right to the tree of life, and may enter in through the gates into the city. [15] For without are dogs, and sorcerers, and whoremongers, and murderers, and idolaters, and whosoever loveth and maketh a lie.

Jesus uses an ancient word for pagans, "dogs." This negative term refers to those who refuse to worship the true God and choose to practice idolatry (see Isa. 56:10; Phil. 3:2).

Some falsely teach that there is no eternal punishment but only final judgment ending in **annihilation**. In these verses, Jesus describes those in the lake of fire, outside new Jerusalem's gates. Unbelievers still exist in an eternal state of suffering and fiery torment.

> **Revelation 22:16** I Jesus have sent mine angel to testify unto you these things in the churches. I am the root and the offspring of David, and the bright and morning star.

Jesus uses an interesting pronoun for this messenger, "mine angel." This glorious angel who reveals much of this prophecy to the apostle John, is the angel assigned to serve Jesus.

Akin explained about the name of Jesus "the offspring of David":

> And this Jesus is the Root (i.e., source) and the Offspring (i.e., descendant) of David (see Isa. 11:1,10). He is before David as God and comes from David as man. He is the root and fruit of David! He is the God-man who is also 'the Bright Morning Star' (see Num. 24:17). The Christology of the end of Revelation is staggeringly high and exalted.[89]

> **Revelation 22:17** And the Spirit and the bride say, Come. And let him that heareth say, Come. And let him that is athirst come. And whosoever will, let him take the water of life freely.

The Holy Spirit within us cries out, "Come." The bride of the Lamb and all the redeemed also cry out, "Come." In the next to last verse of the Bible, John adds his personal call, "Even so, come, Lord Jesus" (Rev. 22:20).

Jesus gives an open invitation, "whosoever will." He invites all those thirsty for salvation to come:

- Salvation is a matter of choice. We cannot choose to save ourselves by our lifestyle of good deeds (Jo. 1:13).

- We all must accept or reject the gift of salvation freely offered by the Lord (Jo. 1:12).

- All those who refuse to come to God through Jesus Christ are lost (Jo. 3:18). All those who believe Jesus died on the cross to save them from their sins, and put their faith in him, are forgiven and saved (Jo. 3:16-17).

- All those who heed God's call to "come" are saved (Acts 2:21).

- No one can earn salvation. It is a free gift (Eph. 2:8).

- Those who accept God's free gift of salvation become children of God (Jo. 1:12)

- Those who become believers become God's children, join Jesus forever in eternal life (Rom. 8:16-17).

We all come to Jesus as sinners. In our sinner's prayer to God, we admit we are sinners and lost without Jesus. Continuing that prayer, we confess to God our belief that Jesus took our sin to his cross to save us. Closing that sinner's prayer, we ask God to forgive us and give us the gift of salvation through Jesus.

If you have not made your confession to God and called on God to forgive and save you, please do it today (2 Cor. 6:2). None of us know when the events of Revelation will begin (Matt. 24:36). This author and your believing friends or family do not wish you to risk your eternity and put off receiving salvation for another day (Acts 26:28).

> **Revelation 22:18-19** For I testify unto every man that heareth the words of the prophecy of this book, If any man shall add unto these things,

God shall add unto him the plagues that are written in this book: [19] And if any man shall take away from the words of the book of this prophecy, God shall take away his part out of the book of life, and out of the holy city, and from the things which are written in this book.

John wraps up this personal, prophetic message from the Lord with a stern warning about these twenty-two chapters. Those who rewrite God's Word and "add unto these things" should heed this warning. The Lord warns all who purposely mistranslates even one word of the original and "take away from the words." Those who change the scripture or cast aside verses in some new edition of God's Word must consider the possible consequences!

Proverbs 30 declared, "Every word of God is pure: he is a shield unto them that put their trust in him. [6] Add thou not unto his words, lest he reprove thee, and thou be found a liar" (Prov. 30:5-6).

> **Revelation 22:20-21** He which testifieth these things saith, Surely I come quickly. Amen. Even so, come, Lord Jesus. [21] The grace of our Lord Jesus Christ be with you all. Amen.

Lessons from Chapter 22:

- **Jesus expects us to keep His word and fulfill his commands while waiting expectantly for his return. Happiness in this life and blessings enjoyed in eternity are found by those who show him their love by doing what he commands.**

- **Each of us continues down a path toward one destiny or the other. Some, the Lord described as "he that is righteous...," are on a path leading to life with God. Others described as "he which is filthy," are on a path toward eternal separation from God.**

# OUTLINE OF CHAPTER 22

I. TWO REALITIES IN GOD'S PRESENCE

    A.  A River of Life 1-2

    B.  A Relationship of Love 3-5

II. TWO REQUIREMENTS OF GOD'S PROMISES

    A.  Readiness 6-15

    B.  Reception 16-21

# ACKNOWLEDGMENTS

To Pastor Dennis Daniel, who was a great help with the manuscript providing his ministry perspective, pastoral and theological insights. I highly value his expertise in Bible prophecy.

To Heather Wright, for all her textual and grammatical corrections and the best sense of humor.

And to my sons, Aaron and Matthew, for their support and encouragement.

# ABOUT THE AUTHOR

C. DAVID WRIGHT STUDIED UNDERGRAD AT California Baptist University and graduate school at Liberty University. He has served various pastoral roles for 35 years in both California and Florida, as well as the privilege of writing and teaching college courses. For over three decades he has taught verse by verse through Revelation, each time building upon previous study and teaching, and by God's grace leading to this commentary.

# BIBLIOGRAPHY

Akin, Daniel L., *Christ-Centered Exposition Commentary: Exalting Jesus in Revelation*, Nashville: Holman, 2016. [a practical expositional commentary]

Baxter, J. Sidlow, *Explore the Book*, Grand Rapids: Zondervan, 1960. [Bible survey with exposition and application of each book]

Combs, Jim, *Rainbows from Revelation*, Chicago: Tribune Publishing, 1994. [practical exposition]

David, Peter H., *More Hard Saying of the New Testament*, Downers Grove: InterVarsity, 1991. [helpful perspectives on challenging passages]

Duck, Daymond R., *Revelation: God's Word for the Biblically-Inept*, Lancaster: Starburst Publishers, 1998. [practical, relevant guide]

Forbush, William Byron, Ed., *Fox's Book of Martyrs*, Grand Rapids: Zondervan, 1926. [originally published in 1563 as *Actes and Monuments*, revised and abridged]

Freeman, James, M., *Manners and Customs of the Bible*, Plainfield: Logos, 1972. [explains many customs practiced in Bible times]

Ironside, H. A., *Revelation*, Grand Rapids: Kregal, 2004. [a devotional commentary]

Ladd, George Eldon, *A Commentary on the Revelation of John*, Grand Rapids: Eerdmans, 1972. [scholarly, comprehensive, technical, expositional commentary]

LaHaye, Tim, *Revelation Unveiled*, Grand Rapids: Zondervan, 1999. [scriptural foundation for the *Left Behind* series]

Lea, Thomas D. and Black, David A., *The New Testament, Its Background and Message*, Nashville: Broadman and Holman, 2003. [a clear and concise introduction to each book of the New Testament]

MacArthur, John, *The MacArthur New Testament Commentary: Revelation 1-11*, Chicago, Moody Press, 1999. [non-technical, comprehensive, practical verse by verse commentary]

——— *The MacArthur New Testament Commentary: Revelation 12-22*, Chicago, Moody Press, 1999.

McGee, J. Vernon, *Revelation-Chapters 1-5*, Nashville: Thomas Nelson, 1991. [from many years of *Thru the Bible* broadcasts]

——— *Revelation-Chapters 6-13*, Nashville: Thomas Nelson, 1991.

——— *Revelation-Chapters 14-22*, Nashville: Thomas Nelson, 1991.

Newell, William R., *The Book of Revelation*, Chicago: Moody Press, 1982. [understandable, comprehensive, verse by verse]

Osborne, Grant R., *Revelation*, Grand Rapids: Baker Academic, 2002. [scholarly, somewhat technical, thoroughly researched, and considered a standard commentary reference on Revelation]

Phillips, John, *Exploring Revelation*, Chicago: Moody Press, 1987. [understandable yet scholarly commentary]

Reed, David A., *Jehovah's Witnesses Answered*, Grand Rapids: Baker Book House, 1986. [good resource written by former JW elder]

Ryrie, Charles C., *Revelation*, Chicago: Moody, 1996. [understandable, verse by verse commentary]

Stedman, Ray C., *God's Final Word*, Grand Rapids: Discovery House, 1991. [practical verse by verse commentary with good application]

Symons, G. J. Ed., *The Eruption of Krakatoa*, London: Harrison and Sons, 1888. [reprint of scientific report on the eruption]

Tozer, A. W., *Jesus is Victor*, Camp Hill: Wingspread, 2010. [compilation of sermons, practical application]

Walvoord, John F., *The Revelation of Jesus Christ*, Chicago: Moody Press, 1966. [an excellent, comprehensive resource on Revelation by an authority on eschatology]

Wiersbe, Warren W., *Be Victorious*, Colorado Springs: David C. Cook, 1985. [practical, understandable commentary on Revelation]

Wilmington, Harold L., *Wilmington's Guide to the Bible*, Carol Stream: Tyndale, 1984. [concise,exhaustive, Bible survey, Bible doctrine, excellent resource]

# Endnotes

1 Ironside, H. A., Revelation (Grand Rapids: Kregel, 2004), 12.

2 Akin, Daniel L., Christ-Centered Exposition Commentary: Exalting Jesus in Revelation, (Nashville: Holman, 2016), 4.

3 McGee, J. Vernon, Revelation—Chapters 1-5, (Nashville: Thomas Nelson, 1991), 43-44.

4 Lea, Thomas D. and Black, David A., The New Testament, Its Background and Message, (Nashville: Broadman and Holman, 2003), 581.

5 Akin, Daniel L., Christ-Centered Exposition Commentary: Exalting Jesus in Revelation, (Nashville: Holman, 2016) 22.

6 Walvoord, John F., The Revelation of Jesus Christ, (Chicago: Moody Press, 1966), 46.

7 Osborne, Grant R., Revelation, (Grand Rapids: Baker Academic, 2002), 98.

8 Baxter, J. Sidlow, Explore the Book, (Grand Rapids: Zondervan, 1960), 341.

9 McGee, J. Vernon, Revelation Chapters 14-22, (Nashville: Thomas Nelson, 1991), 63.

10 Walvoord, John F., The Revelation of Jesus Christ, (Chicago: Moody Press, 1966), 56.

11 McGee, J. Vernon, Revelation—Chapters 1-5, (Nashville: Thomas Nelson, 1991), 70.

12 Osborne, Grant R., Revelation, (Grand Rapids: Baker Academic, 2002), 121.

13  Forbush, William Byron, Ed., Fox's Book of Martyrs, (Grand Rapids: Zondervan, 1926), 9.

14  Phillips, John, Exploring Revelation, (Chicago: Moody Press, 1987), 58.

15  Osborne, Grant R., Revelation, (Grand Rapids: Baker Academic, 2002), 161.

16  Stedman, Ray C., God's Final Word, (Grand Rapids: Discovery House, 1991), 70.

17  Ladd, George Eldon, A Commentary on the Revelation of John, (Grand Rapids: Eerdmans, 1972), 56.

18  MacArthur, John, The MacArthur New Testament Commentary: Revelation 1-11, (Chicago, Moody Press, 1999), 136.

19  Duck, Daymond R., Revelation: God's Word for the Biblically-Inept, (Lancaster: Starburst Publishers, 1998), 58.

20  LaHaye, Tim, Revelation Unveiled, (Grand Rapids: Zondervan, 1999), 113.

21  Ladd, George Eldon, A Commentary on the Revelation of John, (Grand Rapids: Eerdmans, 1972), 82.

22  Akin, Daniel L., Christ-Centered Exposition Commentary: Exalting Jesus in Revelation, (Nashville: Holman, 2016), 124.

23  Ironside, H. A., Revelation, (Grand Rapids: Kregel, 2004), 56.

24  Akin, Daniel L., Christ-Centered Exposition Commentary: Exalting Jesus in Revelation, (Nashville: Holman, 2016), 126.

25  MacArthur, John, The MacArthur New Testament Commentary: Revelation 1-11, (Chicago: Moody Press, 1999), 172.

26  Freeman, James, M., Manners and Customs of the Bible, (Plainfield: Logos, 1972), 471.

27  McGee, J. Vernon, Revelation—Chapters 6-13, (Nashville: Thomas Nelson, 1991), 43.

28  MacArthur, John, Revelation 1-11, (Chicago, Moody Press, 1999), 184.

29  Symons, G. J., Ed., The Eruption of Krakatoa, (London: Harrison and Sons), 1888.

30 MacArthur, John, Revelation 1-11, (Chicago: Moody Press, 1999), 206.

31 Osborne, Grant R., Revelation, (Grand Rapids: Baker Academic, 2002), 294.

32 Reed, David A., Jehovah's Witnesses Answered, (Grand Rapids: Baker Book House, 1986), 104.

33 Freeman, James M., Manners and Customs of the Bible, (Plainview: Logos, 1972), 471.

34 McGee, J. Vernon, Revelation—Chapters 14-22, (Nashville: Thomas Nelson, 1991), 80.

35 Ironside, H. A., Revelation, (Grand Rapids: Kregel Publications, 2004), 84.

36 Osborne, Grant R., Revelation, (Grand Rapids: Baker Academic, 2002), 343.

37 Combs, Jim, Rainbows from Revelation, (Chicago: Tribune Publishing, 1994), 99.

38 McGee, J. Vernon, Revelation–Chapters 6-13, (Nashville: Thomas Nelson, 1991), 106.

39 Osborne, Grant R., Revelation, (Grand Rapids: Baker Academic, 2002), 364-365.

40 Tozer, A.W., Jesus is Victor, (Camp Hill: Wingspread, 2010), 135.

41 Ironside, H. A., Revelation, (Grand Rapids: Kregel Publications, 2004), 97.

42 Ladd, George Eldon, A Commentary on the Revelation of John, (Grand Rapids: Eerdmans, 1972), 143.

43 McGee, J. Vernon, Revelation—Chapters 6-13, (Nashville: Thomas Nelson, 1991), 119.

44 MacArthur, John, The MacArthur New Testament Commentary: Revelation 1-11, (Chicago: Moody Press, 2000), 286-287.

45 Wiersbe, Warren W., Be Victorious, (Colorado Springs: David C. Cook, 1985), 109.

46 Newell, William R., The Book of Revelation, (Chicago: Moody Press, 1982), 150-151.

47  Osborne, Grant R., Revelation, (Grand Rapids: Baker Academic, 2002), 425-426.

48  Wiersbe, Warren W., Be Victorious, (Colorado Springs: David C. Cook, 1985), 111.

49  Osborne, Grant R., Revelation, (Grand Rapids: Baker Academic, 2002), 441.

50  Ironside, H. A., Revelation, (Grand Rapids: Kregel Publications, 2004), 118.

51  Ironside, H. A., Revelation, (Grand Rapids: Kregel Publications, 2004), 138.

52  Ironside, H. A., Revelation, (Grand Rapids: Kregel Publications, 2004), 141.

53  McGee, J. Vernon, Revelation—Chapters 6-13, (Nashville: Thomas Nelson, 1991), 174-175.

54  Akin, Daniel L., Christ-Centered Exposition Commentary: Exalting Jesus in Revelation, (Nashville: Holman, 2016), 236.

55  Osborne, Grant R., Revelation, (Grand Rapids: Baker Academic, 2002), 526-527.

56  Walvoord, John F., The Revelation of Jesus Christ, (Chicago: Moody Press, 1966), 222.

57  Ladd, George Eldon, A Commentary on the Revelation of John, (Grand Rapids: Eerdmans, 1972), 195.

58  Wilmington, Harold L., Wilmington's Guide to the Bible, (Carol Stream: Tyndale, 1984), 432.

59  Ryrie, Charles C. Revelation, (Chicago: Moody, 1996), 105.

60  MacArthur, John, The MacArthur New Testament Commentary: Revelation 12-22, (Chicago: Moody Press, 2000), 117.

61  Stedman, Ray C., God's Final Word, (Grand Rapids: Discovery House, 1991), 273.

62  Akin, Daniel L., Christ-Centered Exposition Commentary: Exalting Jesus in Revelation, (Nashville: Holman, 2016), 256.

63  Walvoord, John F., The Revelation of Jesus Christ, (Chicago: Moody Press, 1966), 246.

64  MacArthur, John, The MacArthur New Testament Commentary: Revelation 12-22, (Chicago: Moody Press, 2000), 147.

65  Wiersbe, Warren W., Be Victorious, (Colorado Springs: David C. Cook, 1985), 146.

66  Stedman, Ray C. God's Final Word, (Grand Rapids: Discovery House, 1991), 285.

67  Ryrie, Charles C. Revelation, (Chicago: Moody, 1996), 118.

68  Ladd, George Eldon, A Commentary on the Revelation of John, (Grand Rapids: Eerdmans, 1972), 224.

69  Akin, Daniel L., Christ-Centered Exposition Commentary: Exalting Jesus in Revelation, (Nashville: Holman, 2016), 264.

70  MacArthur, John, The MacArthur New Testament Commentary: Revelation 12-22, (Chicago: Moody Press, 2000), 161.

71  McGee, J. Vernon, Revelation—Chapters 14-22, (Nashville: Thomas Nelson, 1991), 100-101.

72  MacArthur, John, The MacArthur New Testament Commentary: Revelation 12-22, (Chicago: Moody Press, 2000), 181.

73  Wiersbe, Warren W., Be Victorious, (Colorado Springs: David C. Cook, 1985), 159.

74  Ryrie, Charles C., Revelation, (Chicago: Moody, 1996), 124.

75  Walvoord, John F., The Revelation of Jesus Christ, (Chicago: Moody Press, 1966), 276.

76  Freeman, James M., Manners and Customs of the Bible, (Plainview: Logos, 1972), 37.

77  Osborne, Grant R., Revelation, (Grand Rapids: Baker Academic, 2002), 692.

78  Freeman, James, M., Manners and Customs of the Bible, (Plainfield: Logos, 1972), 472.

79  Akin, Daniel L., Christ-Centered Exposition Commentary: Exalting Jesus in Revelation, (Nashville: Holman, 2016), 298.

80  Walvoord, John F., The Revelation of Jesus Christ, (Chicago: Moody Press, 1966), 306.

81  David, Peter H., More Hard Sayings of the New Testament, (Downers Grove: InterVarsity, 1991), 293-294.

82  Ironside, H. A., Revelation, (Grand Rapids: Kregel, 2004), 196-197.

83  Akin, Daniel L., Christ-Centered Exposition Commentary: Exalting Jesus in Revelation, (Nashville: Holman, 2016), 321.

84  McGee, J. Vernon, Revelation Chapters 14-22, (Nashville: Thomas Nelson, 1991), 160.

85  LaHaye, Tim, Revelation Unveiled, (Grand Rapids: Zondervan, 1999), 363.

86  Osborne, Grant R., Revelation, (Grand Rapids: Baker Academic, 2002), 766-767.

87  McGee, J. Vernon, Revelation Chapters 14-22, (Nashville: Thomas Nelson, 1991), 192.

88  MacArthur, John, The MacArthur New Testament Commentary: Revelation 12-22, (Chicago: Moody Press, 2000), 296.

89  Akin, Daniel L., Christ-Centered Exposition Commentary: Exalting Jesus in Revelation, (Nashville: Holman, 2016), 353.

CPSIA information can be obtained
at www.ICGtesting.com
Printed in the USA
LVHW021749041021
699499LV00008B/375